11/94

How to Manage Your Boss

(2nd Edition)

By
Dr. Roger Fritz

CAREER PRESS
180 Fifth Avenue
P.O. Box 34
Hawthorne, NJ 07507
1-800-CAREER-1
201-427-0229 (outside U.S.)
FAX: 201-427-2037

HOW TO MANAGE YOUR BOSS, 2ND EDITION
ISBN 1-56414-139-X, $9.95
Cover design by A Good Thing, Inc.
Printed in the U.S.A. by Book-mart Press

To order this title by mail, please include price as noted above, $2.50 handling per order, and $1.00 for each book ordered. Send to: Career Press, Inc., 180 Fifth Ave., P.O. Box 34, Hawthorne, NJ 07507

Or call toll-free 1-800-CAREER-1 (Canada: 201-427-0229) to order using VISA or MasterCard, or for further information on books from Career Press.

Library of Congress Cataloging-in-Publication Data

Fritz, Roger.
How to manage your boss / by Roger Fritz. -- 2nd ed.
p.   cm.
Includes index.
ISBN 1-56414-139-X : $9.95
1.Managing your boss. 2. Interpersonal relations.
3. Organizational behavior.   I. Title.
HF5548.83.F75   1994
650.1'3--dc20   94-26666
                                                     CIP

Table of Contents

How to Manage Your Boss

Preface	How to Manage Your Boss	5
Introduction	Is It Possible to Manage Your Boss?	9
Section I	*Know Yourself First*	21
1	Assessing Yourself	22
2	Learning to Manage Yourself	33
3	Managing Your Emotions	41
4	Managing Your Time	57
Section II	*Knowing Your Boss*	67
5	Get Smart: Do You Really Know Your Boss?	69

6	Rate Your Boss as a Manager	85
7	What Are Your Boss's Needs?	97
Section III	*Creating A Climate for Success*	105
8	Your Success is My Success	107
9	Specific Strategies for Success	113
10	Building Better Communication With Your Boss	123
Section IV	*Maintain Your Relationship With Your Boss*	143
11	How You'll Know It's Working	144
12	Manage Your Performance Review	159
13	When It' Not Working	171
Section V	*Do You Know These Bosses?*	177
14	A Gallery of Bosses	180
15	Formal Strategies to Stop Bad Bosses	213
Conclusion	A Final Word	217
	Index	219

How to Manage Your Boss

I'm tired of hearing people complain about bad bosses. It's not that I can't be sympathetic. It's just that I think it's high time they began to initiate action themselves.

This book is about managing your boss. It's not a book for wimps or people not willing to work at it. It's for serious people who are concerned about their careers and committed to improvement.

Since you are now browsing through this copy, I suspect it is safe to assume that you are not one of the legions of passive employees who are content to follow orders and mumble, "Sure, boss...anything you say, boss."

On the contrary. I suspect you are the type who seeks out responsibility, wants to be accountable for your results, and tries to get every last drop of satisfaction out of your job. In short, I'm hoping that you want to make a difference.

If so, *How to Manage Your Boss* will show you how.

By "manage your boss," I don't mean that we're going to turn the tables and let you call the shots in some workplace Sadie Hawkins Day maneuver. I do mean managing *your relationship* with your boss for your mutual benefit—so both of you emerge as winners.

Why your relationship with your boss deserves managing

If you're a parent, you've spent time reflecting on the unique nature of your children and what style of parenting will best meet their needs. If you're a spouse, you have probably figured out the ground rules of your relationship, and know how it should be nourished.

Why, then, shouldn't you devote the same attention to your relationship with your boss? He or she certainly has a lot to do with your future and everything to do with the "happiness factor" at work. Surely this is a relationship worth working on. Don't close your eyes to it or hope it will go away. Manage it!

What if you don't manage your boss?

What if you forget about trying to manage your boss? What will happen if you shrug your shoulders and leave the relationship to chance?

Then you have only yourself to blame. If you just "let things happen" and they get worse, you're stuck.

Boss or wimp?

For our title to be taken literally, your boss would probably have to be a wimp.

Most likely, he isn't. (If he is, he certainly doesn't deserve to be anybody's boss!) Managing your boss is an attention-getting concept, but it isn't intended to be cutesy or disrespectful. Our intent is to help you in specific, practical ways as you initiate action to improve and grow with your current boss and all who follow.

Section I will help you learn more about yourself, so you can understand what you bring to the relationship.

Section II will enable you to analyze your boss's personality and management style, so you will know what kind of an animal you are dealing with.

Section III lays the groundwork for a positive, mutually beneficial relationship that allows you and your boss to achieve your goals.

Section IV gives you pointers on how to maintain the relationship, and tells you what to do when it isn't working.

Section V will help you identify what species of boss you are working with, and give you hands-on strategies for managing your boss.

Expect a bonus

If I am successful in helping you in your quest to build an effective relationship with your current boss, you can expect a big bonus. Maybe it won't be in cash, but the biggest payoff of all will come when it's your turn to be the boss. You will have learned to be a better boss yourself!

In a nutshell:

- This book is for you if you're *restless*. If you're not content with things as they are. If you want to get everything you can from your current position, and then move on.

- This book is for you if you're *persistent*. If you're willing to do what it takes to bounce back from adversity, to prepare for change, to deal with a variety of bosses in tough situations.

- This book is for you if you are *ambitious*. It will point the way for you to plan your career more objectively.

- This book is for you if you're *not afraid of risk*. It is full of strategies and tactics that can help you more effectively manage yourself and your relationship with your boss. None of the strategies are risk-free. Some may even land you in hot water. But every page is devoted to helping you figure out who you are, who your boss is, and what you need to do to be successful *together*.

Introduction

Is It Possible to Manage Your Boss?

Just when you thought you had enough responsibilities at work, someone introduces the idea of managing your boss. "I've got enough to do without having to manage him," you say. "After all, it's his job to manage me. Right?" Wrong!

No matter what your position in a company (unless you own it 100 percent), you will always have a boss. By learning how to manage him, you'll not only make both your jobs easier, you'll build a personal power base that can help you get where you want to go.

A key to making this relationship work better for you both is understanding that management is a two-way street. You must take more responsibility for the flow of information and feedback. It's a growing fact of corporate life in America that the burden for managing the boss-employee relationship should no longer fall entirely on the boss.

It's easy for staff people to feel otherwise. If your boss is weak, unfocused or incompetent, you may want to avoid contact as much as possible. Similarly, when you're working for a boss who keeps dumping work on you, is adversarial in his attitudes or is overly authoritative, it's easy to just "lay low" and hope for improvement.

Usually these approaches are not only counter-productive, they are self defeating. They retard your growth and development, and subtract from the professional image you want to project to others in your company.

The benefits

When you successfully manage your boss, you consciously work with him to obtain the best possible results for the two of you and your company.

Out of that collaboration come several benefits.

1. You create an important professional relationship that can be a rock-solid foundation for your career and your future.
2. You gain the ability to work within the organization, thus gaining resources, support and fair treatment.
3. Because your boss knows you are a dependable and trustworthy ally, you can count on him for support and influence when you have to work with others outside the chain of command.

Managing your boss also provides a more subtle payoff. Most companies have two sets of expectations: expressed and implied. The *expressed* expectations are explained during the job interview, at an orientation and during appraisal meetings. They can be important when they involve your duties and responsibilities; they may be trivial when they convey when it's your turn to make coffee, where you may park.

One of the key issues on the *implied* level is how you handle your relationship with your boss. Do you size up situations quickly and take responsibility for managing them, or turn over the entire matter to your superior?

How an employee handles a boss is very revealing, especially in the first few months on a job. Management keeps its eye on those who show an ability to define and fulfill their own and their boss's expectations. Those who only grumble about their bosses tend to lose favor quickly. The key is to consider each new boss as a challenge, and prove that you can achieve desired results with him.

Clearly, by learning to manage your boss well, you can attract the attention of bigger bosses and pave the way for other moves, onward and upward. *Making your boss look good makes you look good.* There is no substitute for shared accomplishment.

In short, learning to manage your boss is the key to your own promotability.

Are you a proactive employee?

- A proactive employee doesn't wait for the boss to make every move.
- A proactive employee seeks information and the help needed to do the job.
- A proactive employee gives the boss feedback and asks questions.
- A proactive employee initiates action without having to be supervised.

The risks and pitfalls

Managing your boss is an honest, above-board process that you can be proud of. It is not manipulative, nor is it something shady that you may be "caught" and punished for.

But there are risks in trying to manage your boss. Bad and vindictive bosses, for example, may not only resist your attempts to manage them, they also may try to squelch your career.

The silver lining is that if you find that you are working for an unmanageable boss, you will discover that you can't afford to do so and will find the strength you need to make a change. Far better than doing nothing, and finding yourself stuck with a boss who drags you down or hinders your growth!

Four steps to success

Four basic steps are required to build a good relationship with your boss:

1. Conduct an honest self-appraisal of your own needs, objectives and working style, so you can learn to manage *yourself* better.
2. Gather detailed information about your boss's goals, strengths, skills, weaknesses, preferred work style and pressures he is working under.
3. Create a relationship that fits both of your key needs and styles.
4. Take time to maintain the relationship. Keep your boss informed of your feelings and expectations, especially as they change.

In the following pages, these four basic steps will be examined in detail and you'll learn to identify different management styles. Your relationship with your boss can have far-reaching consequences that affect not only your future, but your company's future as well.

In Section V, "Do You know These Bosses?" specific scenarios will give you ways to work through a relationship with a boss who might have seemed impossible until now.

Managing your boss will give you an increased awareness of your role and your boss's role—how they're alike and how they differ. And, who knows, you might even find out that your boss isn't such a bad person after all.

Before you begin these four steps, however, you need to grasp the top-down nature of a typical corporate pyramid, and how its pathways of power can influence the relationship between you and your boss.

The power pyramid

Whether your company has one boss and one employee or one CEO and 800 employees, there's a power pyramid at work: The big boss is at the capstone giving orders and the employees are at the base executing them.

The pyramid as a model for modern corporate structure originates in military history—Caesar's legions and Napoleon's Imperial Army. During World War II, it became the ideal way to pattern work relationships. The CEO at the top fulfilled the same role as a five-star general, and the workers at the bottom were similar to army recruits.

By tracing the job titles downward in the following list, you can see how authority is delegated from one unit of authority to its logical subordinate in the corporate pyramid. Identify your job title or rank, and place yourself somewhere on this list:

- Chief executive officer
- President
- Executive vice presidents
- Senior vice presidents
- Vice presidents
- Department, regional, product managers
- Managerial, zone supervisors
- Senior supervisors
- First-line supervisors
- Workers

Rank and chain of command

The pyramid works because of two concepts: rank and the chain of command. The lower you go in the pyramid, the less powerful your level or rank.

Except for the CEO at the top and the workers at the bottom, everyone in the corporate pyramid performs the dual tasks of employee and boss. They carry out orders from their immediate boss and issue orders to the strata of employees just beneath them. This is called the chain of command and it's the lifeline that filters key information to all parts of the pyramid. It's also a vital concept underlying most interactions in today's corporate world.

The chain of command works because every employee reports to just one boss. The purpose of the pyramid is to divide both large and small tasks into manageable units that are overseen by the bosses and assembled by the employees.

Even though concepts such as shared authority, empowerment and teaming are becoming more popular, the pyramid structure remains typical. More important, even the newer approaches require increased use of the interactive skills advocated in this book.

Where's the power?

Typically, the higher your rank, the more power you have. Upper-level managers, vice-presidents and executive officers usually have the greatest access to a company's resources and the most responsibility for increasing those resources.

If you're an assistant to someone in the upper-level management, count yourself lucky. You're automatically positioned closer to the playing field where critical decisions are made. But even if your boss is further down on the pyramid, you still have a chance at getting in the game and wielding considerable power.

Boss power

Savvy business analysts have identified several kinds of power, but basically "boss power" can be broken down into two types: the power of the position and personal power. No matter where your boss is on the corporate pyramid, he wields at least one kind of power. Take a few minutes and think about the kind of power your boss relies on.

Power of the position
1. The power to reward: giving promotions, raises or recognition for a job well-done.

2. The power to punish: firing or transferring an employee, putting someone in charge of dead-end projects.

3. Authority: can be specifically granted, like the right to sign checks, or can come with the position.

Personal power

1. Expertise: having special skills, knowing a function better than anyone else in the company.

2. Referent power: charm, charisma, integrity and other attributes that makes others want to be like you.

3. Association: who one knows, being in the right clubs and social groups, marrying the right people.

The first three kinds of power come with the territory. The second three could belong to anyone at any level in the organization—a computer wizard who can handle a crashing system and get it back on line, or a charming middle manager who gives speeches for local volunteer organizations.

It's rare when someone possesses all six kinds of power. Bosses are human, too—long in some suits, short in others. Often a boss who is effective and powerful in one area does not even choose to compete in another. Probably everyone has had the experience of working for the boss's son or daughter who possesses plenty of associative power but is lacking in technical expertise. What about the highly demanding boss who threatens, challenges or competes with employees and makes no claim on personal charm? Review the power list above and ask yourself these questions:

1. What kind of power does my boss possess?

2. Could he use it more effectively?

3. Can I convey that to my boss?

4. What kind of power does my boss need?
5. Can I help my boss get that power?

Rank is not the only source of power.

It's important to keep in mind that the power of position or rank can sustain many bosses for a long time. In most corporate structures, employees quickly learn that no matter how incompetent, lazy or disorganized their bosses may be, they are obeyed because of rank—and rank only. Rank can be so influential that in some companies, complaining about your boss to his boss can be corporate suicide. The more top-down the structure of your company, the more you're expected to work with your immediate boss, to carry out his orders and be a team player. Executing your boss's orders is the number-one rule.

Yet, even if you're stuck with an incompetent boss in a highly structured company, don't give up! You still can wield a great deal of power.

Your power

Employees have the ability to make their bosses look like kings or fools. They can withhold vital information, give their bosses poor feedback, or break the chain of command and route projects through other bosses. Dangerous? Yes— but sometimes absolutely necessary for your boss's sake, as well as your own.

In traditional top-down corporations, employees carry out the orders their bosses give them. Bosses seem to have all the power and authority—but they don't! Employees can significantly undermine their bosses' authority without detection: by allowing them to make preventable mistakes, by not meeting deadlines for reports, by blaming others when things go wrong, by spreading false rumors, by "forgetting" to pass on vital information, or by not sharing expertise. In hundreds of ways, staff members demonstrate to associates and even other bosses that their boss has no real power over them.

Eventually, however, these tactics become unsuccessful and will trip you up. They demonstrate behavior that's unprofessional and demeaning to both you and your boss.

There are better ways you can "manage upward" and exercise your power in a positive manner. Let's look at some of the same types of boss power we discussed earlier and apply them to you. Identify which kinds of power you use in dealing with your boss.

The power of the position

1. The power to reward: making your boss look good, getting him out of a jam, giving good feedback.
2. The power to punish: programming your boss for failure, withholding information.
3. Authority: belonging to organizations with negotiating power like labor unions, political coalitions.

Personal power

1. Expertise: being a staff-level expert with a high degree of knowledge in a specialized area, knowing a function better than anyone else in the company.
2. Referent power: charm, charisma, integrity that endears you to others; easy to talk to; makes others want to be like you.

3. Association: who one knows, being in the right social groups, going to the right schools, marrying the right people.

How to use your power

Employees with a certain amount of personal power must be careful not to abuse it. An employee with an MBA from a better school than the boss, or one married to the CEO's daughter, could make a middle-management boss either resentful or anxious to transfer the employee to another department.

Never underestimate your power—no matter how insignificant your position.

Using the power you have to help your boss and the organization shows your boss you understand the value of teamwork. Review the power list above and ask yourself the following questions:

1. What kind of power do I possess?
2. Could I use it more effectively?
3. What kind of power do I need that I don't have?
4. Can I ask my boss to help me get it?

The key to using your power as an employee is to do the best job you possibly can in your present position. Employees who make no secret of their boredom with their middle-management boss, believing their destiny lies in the boardroom, will be left in the dust by the smarter people whose bosses have found them reliable, eager and helpful.

Ideas to build on

The ability to manage your relationship with your boss is a key ingredient of your success on the job. Management notices and promotes people who are proactive—who can define and fulfill their own expectations as well as those of their boss!

The power pyramid is still the basis of most corporate structure, built on the dual concepts of rank and chain of command. You and your boss each have certain powers: the power of the position, and personal power. You can wield similar types of power—either positively or negatively—to make your boss look good or bad.

Learn to play your position well. Being willing to work with your boss is the number-one rule. You can't stay on the sidelines and win!

Power comes in managing the relationship.

Section I

Know Yourself First

A good working relationship with your boss begins with you. The next four chapters will help you make an honest self-appraisal of your own needs, objectives and working style.

Chapter One

Assessing Yourself

The first step in learning to manage your boss is learning to manage yourself.

You may already be knee-deep in handling the responsibilities of your job, with little time, energy or motivation left over at the end of the day. Perhaps you're caught between an unsympathetic boss and uncooperative employees, or maybe your situation at work couldn't be better. In either case, it's important to make a clear assessment of yourself, your skills and your emotional makeup—so you can draw up goals for your personal and career growth.

The steps of self-assessment

Assessing your strengths, weaknesses, skills and strategies is one of the most difficult but productive exercises you can undertake to become a more effective manager of your boss. (It must be tough, because so few people do it!) Having an objective understanding of who you are allows you to accept the parts you like and work on changing the ones you don't. It also makes it easier to separate your boss's constructive feedback from her unwarranted criticism.

These four steps are essential to self-assessment:

1. Understanding your work habits.
2. Understanding your strengths and weaknesses.
3. Setting up goals for improvement.
4. Monitoring your progress.

If you are not willing to start with yourself, forget about getting promoted. It's not likely to happen. And if it does, it won't last long.

What are your work habits?

You may have just started in a new position or perhaps you've been at your job so long you could do your work in your sleep. Has the grind gotten to you, or do you look at each day's challenges as uniquely different? You can find out where you stand by answering these questions. Be sure to give honest, accurate, and recent examples.

- Am I dependable?
  Recent examples: _____

  _____

  _____

- Do I take pride in my work?
  Recent examples: _____

  _____

  _____

How to Manage Your Boss

- Do I steer clear of destructive office politics?
  Recent examples: _____

  _____

  _____

- Do I try to learn from my mistakes?
  Recent examples: _____

  _____

  _____

- Do I approach problems as an opportunity to learn new skills?
  Recent examples: _____

  _____

  _____

Dependability means being at work on time, sometimes arriving early and staying late, meeting deadlines, keeping your promises. Your behavior sets an example to those both below and above you on the corporate ladder. Even a somewhat lazy and disorganized boss will improve her performance when she knows she has conscientious, talented employees on her team who are prepared for meetings.

Pride in your work sends another clear message to your boss and colleagues. Working by the project, not by the clock, means that if necessary, you're willing to dedicate time after work and on weekends to see that a project is done right and deadlines are met. No matter how long you've been in the same position, sloppiness and laziness are not acceptable.

To give your sense of dedication a boost:

- Find new approaches to doing your job.
- Ask for training on new technology.
- Job-share your present position with someone else in the company.
- Attend a motivational seminar.
- Find out how people in similar positions innovate in their jobs. Do this in other companies as well as your own.
- Explore the possibility of using your knowledge and experience to train for a new job within the company.

Above all, *steer clear of harmful office politics*—spreading malicious gossip and rumors. When you're in a managerial position, office rumors can be an important way of obtaining information you may otherwise be denied. But it's crucial to keep a professional attitude and to be supportive of fellow workers—especially your boss.

To monitor your work habits and make sure you are working at peak productivity, devise a check list that ranks all your job duties in order of importance. Revise it weekly to make sure you are touching all your bases, but focusing primarily on your most important tasks.

All resourceful people learn from their mistakes and approach problems as opportunities to learn new skills.

What are your strengths and weaknesses?

Take an hour or so to reflect on your activities in the last year. Ask yourself this question:

What were my major achievements (results) in the past year and how were they related to my objectives?

Start your self-appraisal by using a clean sheet of paper to set up an evaluation form like the one shown on page 27.

Objectives

In this column, you will list, in order of their priority, the goals that you and your boss agree that you were to accomplish in the last year.

Example A: *Add at least 4 new accounts averaging $100,000 with profit margins of at least 22%.*

Example B: *Increase production by 12% with 10% less down time and 5 fewer people by mid-year.*

Measurements used

In this column, list the methods you use to measure your progress toward the agreed-upon objectives. They may involve quantity, quality, time or cost. In Example A:

- The *quantity* factor is 4 new accounts.
- The *quality* factors are $100,000 in sales and 22% profit.
- The *time* factor could be one new account per quarter.
- The *cost* factor could be staying within the approved budget.

In Example B:
- The *quantity* factor is 12% production increase.
- The *quality* factor is 10% less downtime.
- The *time* factor is mid-year.
- The *cost* factor is 5 fewer people.

SELF-APPRAISAL INVENTORY

What were my major achievements (results) in the past year and how were they related to my objectives?

OBJECTIVES	**MEASUREMENTS USED**	**ACHIEVEMENTS**
In priority order, what did my boss and I agree that I was supposed to get done?	Quantity, Quality, Time, Cost #, $, %, +, -	How did I do in meeting my objectives?

1. _____ _____ _____

   _____ _____ _____

   _____ _____ _____

2. _____ _____ _____

   _____ _____ _____

   _____ _____ _____

3. _____ _____ _____

   _____ _____ _____

   _____ _____ _____

4. _____ _____ _____

   _____ _____ _____

   _____ _____ _____

5. _____ _____ _____

   _____ _____ _____

   _____ _____ _____

Achievements

In this column, write out how you did in meeting your objectives. If you didn't complete them, why not? Did your boss have advance warning that your goals would not be met? Were the reasons you didn't meet them controlled by you? If not, why not? For more insights, answer these questions.

- What major dissatisfactions do you have with your performance during the past year? Does your boss agree? If not, why not?

_____

_____

_____

- What are your most important assets in performing the job you now hold? Does your boss agree?

_____

_____

_____

- On a scale of 1 (poor) to 10 (excellent), rate your chances of being selected for your present job if you had to reapply in open competition. Why?

_____

_____

_____

- Would you want to reapply? If not, why?

_____

_____

_____

- What are the personal development areas in which you most need to improve?

_____

_____

_____

_____

- What have you learned during the past year that will help you in your work in the future? Does your boss agree?

_____

_____

_____

- Other than your present assignment, what would you be well-qualified to do in your company? Do you know what you must do to qualify?

_____

_____

_____

What are your goals?

The best companies have mission statements. So should you. Take time to write down both long-term and short-term goals. Start with the long-term goals, because they will determine your short-term goals. Be as creative as you like. Don't limit yourself by defining goals that can only be achieved at your present job. Long-term goals can relate to work, family, hobbies and recreations—any part of your life you want to seriously develop. Your list could look something like this:

1. Be a better parent, spend more time with my children.
2. Finish documentation project for new computer system at work.
3. Improve my tennis game.
4. Research family history.
5. Improve communication with my boss. Seek clarification of her expectations and identify a method of evaluation.
6. Write a romance novel.
7. Identify ways to become more innovative and demonstrate leadership at work.
8. Become my company's first woman vice president.

Now, prioritize the list. As much fun as writing a romance novel would be, chances are it's going to be outranked by finishing the documentation project at work. Yet spending more time with your children and spouse is clearly an important consideration. Better time management and constant reprioritizing and delegating small tasks could free up some time and energy to spend with the family.

Look for the fundamental issues: your commitment to your family; the need for advancement and recognition at work; a desire to take on a creative project; etc. It is important that you understand what issues are basic to your life and their priority. This understanding will help you resolve conflicts with yourself, at home and at work.

For instance, you are offered a promotion at work, but the new job requires a significant amount of travel. This means you would spend much less time with your spouse and children. What do you do? Do you accept or decline the offer? The answer depends on the way you've structured your priorities. Here is a series of questions you can ask yourself to help resolve family/career conflicts:

1. What are my career goals?
2. How have they changed in the past few years?
3. What are my goals for my family?
4. How have they changed in the past few years?
5. Do my actions interfere with progress toward realizing these goals?
6. What elements in my life are in conflict with my career goals?
7. Is the position I currently hold really the best one for me?
8. Am I afraid of failing to meet my goals?
9. Am I afraid of meeting my goals?
10. Am I prepared to adjust my career ambition?

These questions may prove difficult to answer, but you will feel more comfortable with your decision if you've clearly defined and prioritized the fundamental issues in your life.

Short-term goals are the stepping stones that help you reach long-term goals. To achieve better communication with your boss and throughout the department, you could set up monthly short-term goals. For instance:

1. Establish a method for passing on information to my boss. Make sure my boss is passing on vital information to me that she has received from upper management. If necessary, remind her that good communication allows us both to do our jobs better.

2. When appropriate, schedule weekly meetings between staff and management to keep projects on schedule.

3. Solicit feedback from staff regarding the effectiveness of meetings. Ask for ways to help make their jobs easier. Is there training or technical information they need? Are the meetings helpful?

Are you monitoring your progress?

To make sure the goals you set are accomplished, not forgotten, ask yourself these questions every six months:

- How well have I performed in my overall goals?
- Were my goals worth achieving?
- Were my goals worth achieving for my company?
- Based on these answers, what new goals would produce gain for me and my company?

Ideas to build on

Assessing your own performance in the workplace can help you pinpoint strengths you can develop and weaknesses you need to overcome. A solid sense of your abilities, coupled with clear goals and objectives, can help you focus on what you bring to your relationship with your boss—and what you hope to get out of it.

You may think this is all too formal. You may not want to take the time to do it. You may prefer to just wait and see what happens. After all, you're not in serious trouble. Things are going fine. There is no reason to believe your chance to advance isn't equal to everyone else's.

Chapter 2

Learning to Manage Yourself

Managing well is not a skill easily mastered. Good managers generate confidence by demonstrating that they can achieve desired results by bringing out their own best efforts as well as those of their employees. They often teach others by the examples they set. Their validity and credibility as leaders become apparent in the way they conduct themselves day in and day out. Employees watch their bosses to see how they deal with the four big testing grounds of a manager's mettle:

1. How they set goals.
2. How they deal with emotions.
3. How they handle stress.
4. How they manage time.

Managing yourself

The first step in learning to manage yourself is to stop thinking of your work responsibilities as duties and start thinking of them as objectives. *Duties* imply that you're a passive worker waiting to be handed your next assignment. *Objectives* show your boss you're an active, take-charge person.

That's because objectives are the means of attaining results. Results determine progress, progress determines survival, and survival precedes excellence. For example, your company's objective may be to become the leading company in a certain market segment. In order to reach it, you will have to set and meet a number of intermediate objectives, such as doubling next year's sales or halving the product delivery time.

Once these objectives are clear, share them with your boss. Ask for feedback. Make sure you both clearly see the direction in which you're headed, and agree on the need to assess your objectives regularly. Once your boss knows you're serious about self-management, she will be less likely to bother you with petty supervisory tactics.

Begin managing yourself by following these four steps:

1. Define your objectives, measure your performance.
2. Prioritize your responsibilities.
3. Be flexible.
4. Become a team player and build trust.

Define objectives, measure performance

Start by writing down your personal and work-related objectives in one column and how you will achieve these objectives in another column. Performance measurement should include short-term (daily or weekly) and long-term (monthly, annual) evaluations.

To manage yourself more effectively, review your objectives regularly. Once these are clear, it's easier to identify any problems you may have that interfere with managing your boss.

Prioritize your responsibilities

Another effective management tool is learning how to prioritize. Managers rarely have responsibilities or projects that don't overlap.

Write down everything you do over a week's time, then take a look at tasks that are routine, yet time-consuming. If possible, delegate these tasks. Opening the mail, for instance, and tagging the important correspondence can usually be handled by a secretary or an assistant. No matter how few employees you have to rely on, you can always delegate a certain number of tasks. Ask yourself how many of the duties in the following list could be accomplished by an employee:

- Return less important telephone calls.
- Compose standard memos.
- Proofread documents done by word-processing department.
- Prepare conference room for meetings: supply clients with writing supplies, agendas, etc.

If delegating to an employee is not an option for you, try handling your mundane tasks in less time-consuming ways.

- Combine tasks: Open mail while returning phone calls, placing conference calls.
- Plan ahead. When preparing a conference room will interfere with other more important tasks, assemble supplies beforehand.

- Just say "no"—politely. If your boss asks you to interrupt important work to do a less important task, find a diplomatic way to make her see your priorities your way. (Usually your priorities support hers, so remind her of your mutual priorities. Offer to do the other task later.)

When you prioritize, your boss will get the picture that you have work under control. She'll be impressed by your professionalism.

Learn to look at the big picture and decide what's really important for you to do for your boss. The higher your boss rises in the company, the more she'll be deluged with trivial paperwork. You can help her free up her time by keeping your eye on your targeted professional objectives. Some of these may be:

- Consistently complete tasks and projects on time.
- When possible, learn to relay information through group meetings rather than numerous meetings with individuals.
- Establish a relationship with a mentor. This could be your boss.
- Take the initiative when you see work that needs to be done or problems that need to be solved. Don't wait for your boss to point them out.
- Advertise your accomplishments by getting a story in the company newsletter or community publications.

By accomplishing these objectives in a proactive way, you'll not only position yourself favorably with your boss, you'll get a feeling for how she prioritizes her objectives. You might even be able to help her prioritize.

Be flexible

Just as prioritizing is essential, it's also important to be flexible when changes occur. It may appear, at first glance, that your boss is incapable of making a decision and sticking to it. However, her actions could be determined by behind-the-scenes action you have no knowledge of. Deadlines are often delayed and sometimes whole projects are abandoned while new ones are substituted.

When your boss tells you it's time to switch gears or directions, you can remain in charge by being flexible. Realize that it's the nature of things to change—especially in corporate America. Be able to accept new schedules, adjust your objectives and move forward actively. By accepting change, you'll not only demonstrate your professionalism, but you'll make your boss's job a lot easier.

Change means opportunity.

Savvy employees know that change opens opportunities to move upward in their organization. Whether your company is undergoing a merger or your department is getting new office furniture, show that you're able to deal with delays and uncertainty. Don't rigidly cling to old game plans. Instead, make up new ones. Seize opportunities by being receptive to your boss's new strategies. Even with a boss who frequently changes her mind, don't throw in the towel. Throw your support behind the new game plan, have fun with it and plan to stick to it—until things change.

Become a team player and build trust

The ability to cooperate with others is the prime requirement for most jobs. It shows your associates that you're not playing the game to achieve your own ends but for the good of the company. How can you build better team skills?

First of all, whether you're managing employees or simply managing yourself, make sure that group goals and objectives are clearly defined and communicated. A corporate team is not much different from a sports team. You might even find that your boss has used some of the following football strategies in corporate team-building.

- Perceive the goal.
- Devise a strategy on how to reach it.
- Motivate the team to do it.
- Prepare to counteract attempts to prevent it.

Keep in mind that one of your group's constant needs is to forge better interpersonal relationships—a payoff of teamwork that builds mutual trust among employees and identification with the company. An important (and often surprising) aspect of interpersonal relationships is that the more a strong individual sacrifices for the good of the team, the more his or her strengths are appreciated and acknowledged.

It's important for employees to know their bosses trust them to do their jobs without being overly supervised. Persuade your boss to assign open-ended tasks. She'll be relieved of extra work and simultaneously demonstrate her confidence in your ability to act independently.

Trust fosters better relationships both up and down the corporate ladder.

- Trust encourages a better flow of information.
- Trust allows greater creativity.
- Trust promotes acceptance of individuals for who they are.

A good manager's job is very similar to a good parent's or a good coach's. A boss who is able to coach knows how much supervision employees require. And once a player knows the goal and game plan, a coach's job is to let him or her perform. If your boss is a good coach, she'll let you carry the ball and win the game. Show your boss you trust her to let you do a good job. And then do it.

Ideas to build on

Organizations are made one generation at a time. Nothing on this earth lasts. Anyone who truly cares about tomorrow will prepare for it. It wasn't raining when Noah built the ark!

What you do now about managing yourself is the first step in determining how you will manage your boss. Don't miss today's opportunities! Define your objectives and measure your performance.

- Prioritize your responsibilities so you can better manage your efforts and show your boss that your work is under control.
- Be flexible about change and look for the opportunities it presents.
- Build and practice better team skills.

Managing Your Emotions

Emotions and stress can seriously derail your efforts to effectively manage your boss. How you overcome them will have a lot to do with how effectively you interact, not only with your boss, but with co-workers and other employees. To check your usual behavior tendencies, ask yourself the following questions. Try to answer using recent examples that help you determine how serious each issue is.

- Do I become visibly irritated over poor planning and tight deadlines?

_____

_____

_____

_____

How to Manage Your Boss

- Are relationships with my colleagues and boss complicated by unresolved issues in my life (insecurity, need for approval, conflicts with authority)?

_____

_____

_____

- Do I have the resources to get the job done right?

_____

_____

_____

- Am I constantly battling stress?

_____

_____

_____

No matter how professional your outlook or how great your expertise, if you answered "yes" to any of these questions, chances are you could be alienating your boss.

Let's take a look at how emotions influence how others see you.

How many times has this happened to you? A boss you respect highly suddenly loses all control one afternoon and pounds his fists on his desk, berating a trembling secretary. Or a boss you admire for his ability to function under pressure is found screaming over a minor addition to his workload. Even if you empathized with your boss, this loss of control probably made you see him in a new light.

Emotions can be volatile or chilling. They can make us explode with anger or droop from depression. No matter what their nature, the effect of emotions on our energy is draining—whether it's through the rush of a temper tantrum or gradual withdrawal because of guilt or fear.

It's best to know what kind of emotions you experience on a daily basis. See if any of the following statements describe you:

1. I hide or suppress my annoyance with others.
2. I am frequently bored.
3. I can't concentrate on my work.
4. I feel pressured from all directions.
5. I avoid involving others in decision-making and planning.
6. When I become angry, I feel guilty afterward.
7. I frequently worry about trivial matters.

If you answered "yes" to any of these questions, you may have problems handling one or more of the six basic emotions:

Anger	Depression
Joy	Trust
Fear	Anxiety

Everyone feels these emotions with some degree of intensity. They're only a problem when they keep us from performing our jobs—whether it's as a good employee, effective parent or happy, fulfilled adult.

Anger and depression

Some emotions funnel naturally into others. Unexpressed anger can lead to depression; unexamined fear can result in a heightened level of anxiety. Your performance at work will improve—your whole life will improve—when you're aware of your feelings and know how to deal with them. If you answered "yes" to statements one and six on the previous page, you're experiencing anger.

Surprisingly, feelings are often controlled by thoughts. Negative thoughts lead to depression, just as fearful thoughts lower self-esteem. Learning to monitor your negative thoughts is the first step to getting control of your emotions.

If you were to ask most people if they are angry, they would probably deny it. But here are some symptoms of un-acknowledged anger:

- Tense, tight muscles.
- Speaking in a loud voice.
- Knot in stomach.
- Nervous mannerisms.
- Quick, shallow breathing.
- Increased heart rate.

You must decide whether to be the slave or master of anger

People can suppress anger and bottle it up or express it in uncontrolled outbursts; but either way, anger is a particularly potent emotion. Unfortunately, it can also lead to high blood pressure, migraines, ulcers, teeth-grinding and depression. Unexpressed or poorly expressed anger can damage your relationship with your boss and fellow employees, because they will sense your latent hostility and feel defensive. You must decide whether to be its slave or master.

Your feelings of anger, particularly with your boss, might be justified. Perhaps you have a boss who likes to deliberately upset and frustrate employees. Take your "emotional temperature" and see if you have any unresolved feelings of anger toward your boss. Try to be objective and determine if they're justified. If so:

- Clearly point out to him what he's doing that causes your angry reactions.
- Suggest possibilities for change.

If he's not willing to change his behavior, you should devise ways to monitor your own reactions before they reach the boiling point by:

- Excusing yourself for a "cooling off" period when discussions become heated.
- Staying in touch with your feelings and giving your boss feedback: "It's difficult for me to follow your instructions when you yell."

If your angry feelings toward your boss seem unjustified or out of proportion, chances are you're dealing with previously unresolved issues of anger. To find out if your anger is chronic, ask yourself:

- Do I lose my temper easily over unimportant trivialities?
- Does my boss's behavior remind me of someone else with whom I'm really angry?
- Is my anger predictable? For example, do I tend to blow up at certain times of the day (after breakfast or lunch when blood sugar is low)?

Find a professional who can help you deal with your anger. It could be getting in the way of your career. When your boss sees you as overly emotional and edgy, he'll hesitate to trust you with important assignments. As much as he values your strengths and abilities, your volatile, unpredictable reactions might make you an undependable team player.

Depression is a feeling of sadness or grief. It can spring from unexpressed anger or stem from an event such as illness, a death in the family or a failure at work. Often people admit they're "angry" at a friend or a family member who has died, leaving them to contend with life on their own.

Depression has few, if any, positive effects. It does tell you something is wrong. When you deny depression, preferring not to examine its cause, it can turn into chronic depression, which lowers your energy level and makes you unable to function.

The most effective way to cure depression is to first identify what's causing it. That can be relatively simple if you are suffering from an isolated case of depression caused by a major change in your life (moving, divorce, illness, etc.).

However, if you are chronically depressed, identifying the source of your depression is more difficult. This type of depression can be driven by numerous complex emotions.

Among them are:

- Low self-esteem.
- Feelings of insecurity.
- Constant need for approval.

If you think you fall into this category of chronic depression, consider talking to a counselor, psychologist, clergy member or a professional who can help you identify and correct the source of your depression.

You may have the world's most empathetic boss—or you may not. But even a supportive boss gets tired of an employee who needs constant re-energizing to get the job done. Depression may cause you to feel like you're completely isolated; however, your energy level affects everyone with whom you work.

To work through your depression you may need more privacy, understanding friends or extra sleep (read *Sleep Disorders: America's Hidden Nightmare,* by Roger Fritz, published by National Sleep Alert). It's unlikely you'll find any of these at work. Make every effort to counter the effects of depression by:

- Getting to work on time.
- Being decisive.
- Taking pride in your work.

Joy and trust

Joy is, or should be, a very real part of our daily lives both at home and at work. It restores our energies and regenerates our view of the world.

One type of power that good bosses have is the power of personality—the ability to inspire others with enthusiastic leadership. Managers who lack joy are not inspirational. Worse yet, they infect employees with their own defeatism. By the same token, listless employees can make their boss's jobs much tougher, if not impossible. The effects of joy in the workplace are limitless. It can:

- Motivate employees to participate in consuming, goal-oriented work.
- Promote sharing, generosity and teamwork.

How to Manage Your Boss

- Allow employees to substitute the pleasures of discovery for the dull patterns of habit and routine.

Easier said than done, you may say. Your only joy in your dull job may come at 5 p.m. on Friday afternoon when you're facing a work-free weekend. If so, evaluate what you're doing. If you have tried your best and can't find a way to improve your job or your spirits, move on to something more fulfilling. If your outlook is decidedly joyless but your work still offers some reward, it may mean your self-esteem is at an all-time low. Here are four ways to boost it:

1. Avoid comparing yourself to others. Your achievements and abilities are unique.
2. Reward yourself.
3. Accept praise and accent the positive. Don't dwell on past mistakes.
4. Ask those who love you to help you build on your strengths.

If you have tried your best and can't find a way to improve your job or your spirits, move onto something more fulfilling.

Joy fuels you with added energy. It allows you to work hard, acting with confidence and decisiveness, pushing projects through to their final conclusion.

Whether you love your job or simply find it pays the bills, every boss wants enthusiastic players on his team. Your joy and pride in your work are infectious. They can enliven fellow workers and even a dull boss.

Self-trust

We've mentioned trust as a part of teamwork, but it's so essential, it's worth mentioning again. Without trust, the corporate world would no longer exist. It's the glue that binds all relationships and agreements. Your trust in others can be limited by how much you trust yourself. Here are four ways to improve your self-trust:

1. View yourself as unique. Don't try to fit into a mold.
2. Listen to your "inner voice."
3. Welcome responsibility.
4. Be spontaneous: Follow your intuition in approaching a task or problem. Don't stay in a rut.

Self-trust gives you several distinct advantages on the job:

1. It allows you to recognize and rely on your abilities. It gives you confidence to cope with difficult situations.
2. It provides you with the inner strength to act decisively and push for results that may lack popular support.

If you find yourself relying too much on the rules, unwilling to delegate tasks, suffering from disorganization or supervising your employees' work too closely, you need to improve your trust in others and in yourself.

Trust begets trust. The more confident and self-trusting you are, the more you will trust your boss to do his job. He, in turn, will recognize your support by showing his trust in you. He'll trust you to play by team rules, do the best job you can and handle difficult assignments. Mutual trust among employees and employers allows you to bypass time-consuming red tape, cumbersome rules and regulations. Once trust is established, both you and your boss will be more innovative, and your jobs will be more fun.

Fear and anxiety

Fear is one of the most basic emotions known to humans. It prompts the body to pump adrenaline in anticipation of the classic "fight or flight" situation. We experience fear almost daily, yet not many people would admit to being fearful. It simply doesn't go with the confident image demanded by the corporate world; yet we're all afraid of making mistakes, of displeasing our bosses, of losing our jobs.

**When fear goes unexamined, it can
produce a high level of anxiety**

Some people are afraid of not "fitting in"—of how business associates would regard them if they acted slightly different, or if their true natures were known. Some of those who have made it to top-level management jobs suffer from the impostor syndrome: They have constructed a professional "persona" that conforms to others expectations. They are actors and actresses.

A person in this situation may feel he or she has to be tough with employees to appear strong, or become a workaholic and forego spending time with family to conform to a hard-driving executive image. Unfortunately, these people often think: "This is not the true me. Somehow this all happened by accident. If others knew the true me I might lose respect, influence or power."

When fear goes unexamined, it can produce a high level of anxiety. Keep in mind it is an emotion that won't simply go away. To deal with fear effectively, you must recognize it then control it to your advantage.

When fear is out of control, it can limit your social and business life, and it can prevent you from functioning effectively.

Ask yourself:

- Do I frequently feel fearful?
- Is fear limiting me in any way?
- Has my fear acted as a self-fulfilling prophecy on several occasions? If so, how?

Some fears are groundless, some are not. If you're afraid of displeasing your boss, try to determine if you're acting out of insecurity or if you have some reasonable motive. Maybe your boss became openly hostile and punitive to other employees who displeased him in the past.

To overcome fear, it helps to rationally identify what you are afraid of, then think of a "worst-case" scenario. Make a realistic evaluation of what is liable to happen. Your list could look something like this:

- Fear: Making mistakes at work.
- Effect: Being ridiculed.
- *Worst outcome:* I become angry, lose control, lose co-workers' respect at work.
- *Realistic evaluation:* Everyone makes mistakes. Reasonable mistakes are generally tolerated where I work. I can learn from my mistakes.

Believe it or not, fear has positive uses in the business environment. It all depends on intensity and duration. Moderate, occasional fear stimulates; continuous fear paralyzes. People are most fearful when they're learning a new job or defending a present one. You can benefit from occasional fear in two ways:

1. It allows you to learn and evaluate new situations quickly.
2. It can stimulate you to develop effective changes, countermeasures and improvements.

**Moderate, occasional fear stimulates;
continuous fear paralyzes.**

The best way to conquer fear is to learn to relax, visualize yourself in a positive situation, and make positive affirmations. Nothing can do more damage to your work performance than being afraid of your boss. You have to ask yourself if your fear is justified or misplaced. Does your boss bully and threaten employees or does your insecurity with your boss's ego make you uneasy?

Some bosses like throwing employees off-center by behaving inconsistently, making unreasonable demands and alternately punishing or rewarding them at inappropriate times. Whatever your boss's behavior, ask yourself:

1. Does he have anything to gain by making me afraid of him? What is it?
2. What do I have to lose by being afraid of him?

Unless your boss is violent, vindictive or deviant, chances are he's testing to see how far you will let him go with his "obnoxious boss act." If you think your boss's bark is worse than his bite, stand up to him. Fear of your boss may be the major hurdle you must overcome. Tell him how his behavior makes you feel; that you'd prefer he monitors it when you're around. He might not change, but may respect you for having the nerve to confront him.

If, however, his bite is worse than his bark, you've got a tough boss to handle. Tough, angry bosses are discussed in Chapter 14.

Anxiety produces feelings of uneasiness and apprehension. Anxiety can result when you are worrying about a future event rather than confronting a present danger. Many people experience anxiety in stress-related situations like these:

- Time pressures to work more quickly.
- Evaluation of your work by your boss.
- Increasing demands or complexity of your job.
- Learning new skills.
- Health problems.
- Inner conflicts between personal values and job responsibilities.
- Coming into contact with a large number and/or variety of people.
- Getting a new job or a new boss.

People experience anxiety when they have to make changes. However, many times these changes are positive. Anxiety can, for instance:

- Motivate you to attack a problem directly.
- Help you analyze a situation.
- Prompt you to set goals, reevaluate your talents and abilities, etc.

No boss likes to work with a worrier. If your boss perceives you as being overly concerned with petty details or taking up his time whining and complaining, his trust in you will erode.

When your anxiety is justified—you've heard rumors, or the company's experienced poor financial performance—ask your boss to verify the information you have. Even if he is not in a position to confirm or deny the bad news, he'll appreciate your letting him in on the grapevine.

Emotional rescue

To get a better grip on your emotions, it's helpful to keep an "emotion diary." Write down what you felt each day, at what time and, if possible, what event, individual or circumstance triggered the emotion. Some emotions, like irritability or depression, are triggered by varying levels in blood sugar occurring just before or after meals.

Notice if a pattern starts to emerge. See if you're easily upset by the success of others, in which case your self-esteem may need bolstering. Check to make sure that the constant headaches, fatigue, colds or flu you're battling really aren't symptoms of depression.

Don't try to wrestle with these emotions on your own. If you're not pulling out of a depression or you can't get control of your anger, it's likely the problem goes back to subconscious patterns learned early in your life. Don't hesitate to seek counseling. A lot of companies have medical insurance that can pay, either wholly or in part, for therapy. When in doubt, go to an expert.

Ideas to build on

To gain control of your emotions:

- Learn to monitor your negative thoughts.
- Take your "emotional temperature" and see if you have any unresolved feelings of anger toward your boss.
- Consider finding a professional to help you deal with anger or depression.
- Take steps to boost your self-esteem and build your self-trust.
- Think of a "worst-case" scenario and a more realistic evaluation for each of your fears in the workplace.
- Keep a diary of your emotions and watch for patterns that you can learn to control.

Chapter 4

Managing Your Time

When 5 p.m. comes, have you completed most of the day's objectives or do you stare at the clock, wondering where the time went?

Managing time effectively is one of the most valued skills you can possess. When you know how to structure your time, you show your boss you're organized and efficient. You also show her that you value time—yours *and* hers—and, as a precious resource, you won't waste it.

If organizing your time is a problem, ask yourself these questions:

- Do I get projects done on time or are they late?
- Do I need to spend more than 40 hours a week in the office?
- Am I willing to forego breaks and lunches to meet a deadline?
- Is my work constantly interrupted by my boss, co-workers, phone calls?

- Do I spend a lot of time at the office in personal conversation?
- Does my boss dump extra work on me? Does she frivolously reassign projects and deadlines to suit her changing schedule?
- Is my style of time management compatible with my boss's style?

Time management strategies

The way you manage time says a lot about the way you manage other aspects of your life.

Do you arrive at work 10 minutes late, wander into the lunchroom for coffee and catch up on the morning's gossip with co-workers? Or do you arrive a little early, directed and focused, with a list of what you plan to accomplish?

If you were the boss, which kind of employee would you prefer working with?

Maybe you'd like to be more like the employee in the second scenario, but getting organized is a problem. Once you're seated at your desk, phones start ringing, people drop by to visit and the day has taken off in a direction all its own. Priorities take the form of crisis management.

One way of gaining control of your time is to make a "to-do" list either before or as soon as you arrive at work:

- Include high, medium and low priorities.
- Work on one project at a time. Don't begin several projects at once.
- Don't take on extra projects until everything on the to-do list is finished.

To avoid interruptions while working on your to-do list, try these simple solutions:

- If you have an office door, shut it.
- Ask the people at the switchboard to hold your calls or put your phone on "do not disturb."
- When co-workers drop by to chat, explain you're busy, then set a time when you can get back to them.

Time management and your boss

Your ideas and your boss's ideas of time management may be directly opposed. Perhaps you're highly organized and your boss prefers to work more casually. Styles don't matter as long as both of you manage to get your jobs done. What does matter is when your respective styles of time management interfere with effectiveness.

Do any of these situations fit your relationship with your boss?

Scenario 1:

Your boss is a stickler for meeting deadlines, commits 50 to 60 hours of her working week to the office. You, on the other hand, enjoy spending time with your family, have outside interests and lots of friends at work.

You think your boss:

- Is too hard-driving.
- Should spend more time with her family.
- Worries too much about job performance; she has her boss's support and can afford to relax more often.
- Interferes too much with your work style; would like you to work from a to-do list every day.

Your boss perceives you as:

- Spending too much time socializing at work.
- Disorganized and unmotivated.
- Lacking in company loyalty.
- Not helping to meet her deadlines.

Scenario 2:

Your working style is dedicated and effective, your boss's style is laid-back. While you like to pre-plan projects and meetings, she takes each day as it comes. You've already planned the vacation you're taking a year from now; your boss may take next week off...she isn't sure yet.

You perceive your boss as:

- Relying on you to organize her.
- Irresponsible and lazy.
- Lacking an overall game plan for the department.
- Standing in your way of possible advancement.

Your boss sees you as:

- Too rigid and obsessive about time-planning.
- Wanting to control her.
- Ambitious and easily frustrated.
- Organized, yet overbearing.
- Not well-liked by associates.

Learn how to offer your time management skills without alienating your boss.

In both scenarios, differing attitudes about time management can lead to real conflict between employee and boss. You may be better organized than your boss—especially if your boss depends on personal power to strengthen her position. Some bosses expect their employees to be better time managers than they are. Learn how to offer your time management skills to your boss without alienating her. The overall goal is to build a strong team and become a better player.

To help get your time firmly under control, construct a time log for the hours you spend at work. Include the time it takes you to dress and drive to work. Try keeping a diary at work that records time in 10-minute segments. Time at work can be allocated to three types of activities:

- Fixed activities: staff meetings, production reviews, administrative matters.

- Semi-flexible activities: routine correspondence, meetings with customers, supervising employees.

- Variable activities: items beyond your control, such as phone calls, visits, personal matters handled during work hours.

Once you know how your time at work is spent, compare it to your short-term goals for the day, for the week. Recognize the link between activities and goals. Each time you undertake an activity, ask yourself the following questions:

- Is this activity leading me toward or diverting me from a larger goal?

- Is it possible to combine activities so that I can free up bigger blocks of time?

Stress: Are you victim or culprit?

Stress is part of daily life and it can become a serious obstacle. Driving in heavy traffic can produce stress; so can winning a marathon. Many Type A high-achievers find pleasure in the slight buzz they experience from so much to do in so little time. It's important to remember that stress can be caused by too many problems or too much success. Either way, your body interprets it as an overload of stimuli and responds by telling the adrenals to kick into high gear.

Defining overload

Stress, when not handled properly, can quickly escalate through various stages, beginning with anxiety and ending in a total inability to function. At this stage, stress is your body's way of saying stop—and it means it.

Stress in the workplace often occurs when you take on too much. You feel it's your job to solve not only your own problems but those of your boss and staff as well. Your overloaded schedule may not kill you, but it can put a damper on your overall outlook on life. A life that is devoted to work—with no time for fun or relaxation—can put you into a state of exhaustion and depression.

Look at what you do. Evaluate how stressful your job is. Think about the issues involved in the discussions on emotions and time management. Unresolved emotional conflicts or poor time management can also add to your level of stress.

Keep in mind that the group with the highest level of stress in America are not overly committed CEO's or hard-driven entrepreneurs—they are clerical workers. The reason? They have very little control over their working lives.

At the bottom of the corporate ladder, they are subject to the whims of various bosses, personnel departments and warring corporate factions in need of their services.

To assess the built-in stress of your position, you need to pin down your own answers to these questions:

- Is my job stressful within itself (high pressure to perform, to meet deadlines)?
- Do I make it more stressful than it need be?
- Does my boss make it more stressful than it need be?
- Do I have any personal power in this position?
- How many bosses must I please?
- Am I meeting overall goals in this position?

As downsized corporations delegate more work to fewer people, many employees are spending 50, 60, even 70 hours a week handling a workload that was once spread among a larger group.

If your company has downsized without reducing the overall workload, your efforts to meet unrealistic expectations about your productivity may wear you out.

These expectations may not all come from your boss. In downsized companies, chances are good that *everyone* is struggling to keep up, your boss included. The time management tactics recommended in this chapter—namely, setting priorities, eliminating routine but time-consuming activities, and delegating what you can—will help you keep your head above the water.

But there are other steps you can take to make sure that overwork doesn't push you over the edge.

1. Stay alert for signs of stress, such as irritability, poor concentration or depression.

2. Find a sympathetic ear, someone who knows what you're going through.
3. Add a little fun to your life by treating yourself to short, enjoyable activities several times a day. Take a few minutes to call a friend, walk around the block, pull up the solitaire game on your computer or solve a few crossword puzzle clues.

How stress affects your relationship with your boss

Even if you and your boss see eye-to-eye, stress still affects your relationship. See if any of these situations fit:

- Your boss loads you down with plenty to do, but after you've met tough deadlines, she fails to recognize your accomplishments.
- Your boss increases your responsibilities, but doesn't give you the resources (position or staff) to accomplish them.
- Your boss explains that you need to manage time more effectively, then derails you in a series of lengthy, pointless meetings.

"Joyless" stress comes from feeling disenfranchised, powerless and overburdened with detailed tasks. Sometimes, to gain more control of your life, you must say "no" to a demanding or dictatorial boss. It can also make you better able to interact with your boss when she realizes that you will not tolerate unreasonable demands.

When your boss discusses a new project that creates potential conflict with existing priorities, don't assume that the new project has a higher priority. Ask first. Ask again. Check around and negotiate to find out just how much emphasis to give the project.

The good, the bad, and the ugly

There's a bad kind of stress and a good kind. You and your boss may both be workaholics who bask in the glow of a high-pressure but rewarding working relationship. See if you two share any of the following examples of "good" stress:

- Passion and enthusiasm for your work.
- Being centered in the present, refusing to dwell on past successes or failures.
- Mutual resourcefulness: You draw upon each other's ability to constructively and imaginatively accomplish goals and create solutions.
- Personal power: Your boss has the power to influence the environment. In turn, she empowers you.
- Perseverance: You have a mutual commitment to innovation.
- Optimism: You're both open to new options and share them as often as possible.
- Goal setting: You're both good at defining specific goals to be accomplished within specific time frames.

Learning to effectively manage your emotions, time and stress is the first step in managing your boss. It shows your boss you mean business and can control stress, without letting it control you.

Ideas to build on

Becoming a better manager of your time shows your boss you're organized and efficient. You can implement various strategies to help gain control of your time:

- Keep a to-do list with high, medium and low priorities.
- Avoid interruptions—phone and personal.
- Assess how you and your boss react to the concept of time management. Are your working styles the same or different?
- Keep logs of how time is spent at work. Start linking *all* activities to goals.

Stress complicates your relationship with your boss. Its sources can be pleasant or unpleasant events, all signifying change of some sort.

It is your responsibility to see how you and your boss create stress for one another. Is it "good" or "bad" stress? How much of it can be avoided through better planning, better communication?

Section II

Knowing Your Boss

Step two in the process of building a good relationship with your boss is getting as much detailed information as possible about his goals, strengths, skills, weaknesses, preferred working style and the pressures he is working under.

The chapters in Section II will help you gather this information. Chapter 6 tells you how to observe behavior and gather the facts you need. Chapter 7 helps you evaluate your boss's management skills. Chapter 8 introduces requirements that every boss has, and helps you pinpoint the specific needs of your boss.

Taken together, this section will help you lay an excellent foundation for a relationship that will benefit both of you!

Chapter 5

Get Smart: Do You Really Know Your Boss?

Knowing yourself is half the battle of managing your boss. Knowing your *boss* is the other half.

Deep down, most people would prefer not having a boss. In many cases the relationship all too closely mirrors the one we had with our parents. Bosses tell us what to do, criticize our work, prioritize our tasks and time, and ultimately decide our future with the company. It's easy to fall into the trap of responding to our bosses the way we did to our parents: like overly compliant good kids or sullen, rebellious teenagers.

Neither kind of behavior earns us a boss's trust. No matter how gruff or intimidating a boss may be, the last thing he needs is an apple-polisher or a terrorist. A good boss welcomes strong employees who aren't afraid to say when a problem exists. But how that relationship develops is mostly up to you.

The first step in managing your boss is to realize your boss is fallible, a human being just like you, with obvious strengths and weaknesses. In this chapter we'll take an objective look at your boss. You'll get to know him, maybe for the first time. More important, you'll learn to use this information to discover his needs. In the next chapter, you'll learn how to make him need you—a guaranteed prescription for a long and healthy career.

To get to know your boss better, you must assess:

- His goals.
- His power.
- His particular strengths and skills.
- How he handles his emotions and responds to the emotions of others.
- His personal style.
- How he handles stress.
- His needs.
- What he's like away from work.

What are my boss's goals?

You spent some time in Chapter 1 defining and prioritizing your goals and objectives. Think how much those goals say about you—where you're headed, what you ultimately want from your career, your family, your life. What if you could take a look at a list of your boss's goals? It would tell you a lot about the individual you're working for.

As soon as you can, ask your boss if he's willing to share a list of work-related goals with you—both short-term and long-term. He may not even have defined them for himself. Or he may prefer to rely on a less-structured approach—by verbalizing goals in project meetings.

Even if your boss hesitates to communicate his goals, you probably are familiar with some of them from your day-to-day contact. List the projects he is in charge of; think about where he wants to go in the corporate structure. Then make a list of his goals. Include what you perceive are his commitments to family, community and favorite recreations. Don't worry about putting them in any particular order. It's more important to rely on your intuition and spontaneity in this exercise. Your list might look something like this:

My boss's goals
1. Get marketing project in on time and under budget.
2. Become a better golfer, or at least find a way to deal with frustration.
3. Keep his boss satisfied and off his back.
4. Spend more time with kids and coach his son in baseball.
5. Spend more time with his wife.
6. Develop a modified projection of sales for the next quarter based on sales figures from branches.
7. Successfully present the new quarterly projection to his boss.
8. Help start a Neighborhood Watch group.
9. Be under consideration for the marketing director position.

When your boss's goals are in conflict

A common source of friction is when your boss has goals that conflict with one another.

To help resolve this conflict, ask him to compare your list with his. Be tactful and diplomatic, and limit your discussion to business goals. (He probably won't be comfortable discussing personal and family goals with you anyway.) By reviewing the list and using your intuition and observations regarding his personal and family goals, you'll be able to spot the problem areas: weekends of number-crunching to project next quarter's sales will eat up valuable time he wants to spend with his family. What kind of additional responsibilities does your boss have? Is he willing to make further sacrifices of time and energy with two small children at home?

Helping your boss solve conflicts like these is a surefire way to meet his needs and yours. Chapter 10 will delve into the details of meeting mutual needs.

Your boss's power

Review the power pyramid in Chapter 1 and see where your boss fits in. Ask yourself what kind of access he has to the following resources:

- Increased budget for staff or supplies.
- Time to devote to company planning.
- Powerful allies in high places.

Getting a clear picture of the resources your boss has gives you a practical understanding of what he can do for his employees.

Now look at the six kinds of power outlined in the Introduction. Evaluate what kind of power your boss brings to his relationship with you and to what degree.

Power of position

1. The power to reward.

Is your boss in a position to give you a promotion or a raise? If so, is it only during an annual review or can he confer immediate raises and bonuses? How does he recognize you for a job well-done?

- *Informal recognition:* an encouraging word, taking you out to lunch.
- *Formal recognition:* company newsletter, memo to others, including you in meetings and seminars.
- *Mentoring:* an acknowledged commitment on his part to take you under his wing to develop your promotability.

2. The power to punish.

Does your boss have the power to fire you?

Does your boss have the power to redefine your job responsibilities or transfer you to another department?

Does he have the capability of undermining you so you'll quit? Could he subvert your authority over your employees?

Could your boss undermine your support from other bosses within the company?

Could your boss damage your credibility by assigning you dead-end or problem projects?

3. Authority

Does your boss's authority come with the position?

How effectively does he use it?

Does he love exerting authority and overrunning his bounds?

Is he afraid to claim it; does he run the risk of losing it?

Personal power

1. Expertise

Is your boss an expert in a particular function: marketing strategy, computer programming, architectural engineering?

Does he share his knowledge readily with others?

Is he grooming someone to take his place?

Does he expect you to easily grasp what only he understands? Is he willing to teach you?

2. Referent power

Does he possess a tremendous amount of charm, charisma and integrity that makes others want to be more like him?

Is he well-known and well-liked throughout the company, community and city?

Does he rely solely on his personality to get others to do his job?

How does he interact with friends and family? In the same manner or differently?

Can his connections help you get where you want to go?

3. Association

Does your boss come from the "right family" or know the right people?

Does his social background help or hinder him in doing his job well?

Does he overlook your strengths because you're not from the same background?

Does your boss have connections by marriage?

Your boss's strengths and weaknesses

Make an honest appraisal of your boss's strong and weak points. Maybe you've been so overwhelmed by his charismatic personality that you've never stopped to realize he's a little short on technical skill. Bosses, just like other people, need help in the areas where they're weakest. If your boss really knows how to motivate his staff but lacks ability to follow through, he may need some organizational help.

Start observing your boss in action and keep a list of how he operates, innovates and motivates others—a kind of "report card" you can update regularly. Remember, the objective is not to indulge in excessive fault-finding but to see your boss in a new light—as a multifaceted human being. Ideally, you'll discover a way to lend your boss a hand, make him look better and forge a stronger working relationship.

Your evaluation could look something like this:

Perceived Strengths

- Manages time efficiently
- Good listener
- Fair-minded
- Good technical background
- Has integrity
- Defends his employees

Perceived Weaknesses

- Doesn't use all the resources available to the department.
- Too detail-minded, loses sight of the big picture and long-range objectives.
- Not perceived as a strong leader within the company.

By comparing what you perceive to be your boss's strengths and weaknesses, you'll get a good feel for where he's effective and where he could use some help. The individual described in the list above has a lot of technical expertise and is a caring, loyal boss who goes to bat for his employees. He's not a charismatic or skillful enough corporate player to claim much of the company's resources, such as a bigger budget for more computer terminals, additional staff or raises. Chances are, his most ambitious employees will want to work for a more powerful supervisor in a department where the heavy-hitters are, and where the stakes are higher.

Attitude makes the difference

It's important to realize that your attitude can enhance both your boss's strengths and his weaknesses. Remember, all bosses are judged by how well they perform for their supervisors and how well they motivate their employees. That's where you come in. Eventually, you'll learn how to help your boss improve his performance. But the best way to start is to show him you're on his side, that you're playing on his team—a team that will make you both winners.

How your boss deals with emotions

Your boss's team-building ability is directly affected by the way he handles his emotions. How does your boss stack up in these areas?

- *Keeping a positive mental attitude.* Perhaps he failed once and is too afraid of failing again to really try.

- *Separating the process from the product.* If his strategies were good but the effort failed, it might not be his fault.

- *Avoiding perfectionism.* The workplace is full of distractions and conflicting priorities that call for compromise and doing the best job possible, then moving on.

- *Learning to understand failure.* Growth and discovery can't take place without failure.
- *Trusting and empowering employees.* They're here to do their jobs as well as possible. The better they are, the better the boss's entire department or product will be.

Depending on how well he deals with his emotions, your boss may fall into an "emotional type"—angry, fearful, or effective. Do any of these types sound familiar?

The angry boss

Some bosses use anger as a means of controlling others, especially their employees. To this person, the advantages of bullying tactics far outweigh the disadvantages that may result from losing control.

Obviously, no one wants to bring an angry boss bad news. Inappropriate anger by a boss shuts down communication and transforms employees from supportive to subversive. When your boss is extremely frustrated, an angry outburst may be justified and can be healthy. Does he express anger appropriately and constructively? Does he play fair? How long does it take for him to recover from his anger? These questions will enable you to determine how anger may be hurting your boss.

- Does your boss keep his remarks impersonal: focused on an action and not personal characteristics?
- Does he refer only to the situation at hand and not dwell on the past, reciting old infractions and mistakes?
- How does he react to an angry employee?

- Does he check his facts to make sure his anger is directed at the right person?
- Does he give someone a chance to explain before he gets angry?
- Does he make it clear why he's angry?
- Does he make threats?
- Does he provide alternatives or solutions?
- Does he discipline employees in private or in front of their co-workers?

Being the object of another person's wrath—especially when it's your boss—is upsetting and frightening. Try to stay objective and see if your boss has a valid reason to be upset.

Some tough, overly aggressive bosses allow no room for error. If this is your boss's style (meaning he tends to threaten everyone this way), it's important not to take his outburst personally. It helps to look for the underlying motive for his behavior. Some possibilities are:

- He believes in the "drill sergeant" approach to motivating others.
- He has a strong need to control and intimidate others.
- He is a highly emotional person. In other words, his enthusiasm is as intense as his negativism.

To see if you're reading your boss right, watch how he interacts with others above, below and beside him.

The fearful boss

Weak bosses often fear their own bosses and envy employees who appear more confident than themselves. A weak boss can sabotage you just as easily as an overly aggressive boss. Rather than ignoring weak and fearful bosses and hoping they just fade away, it's best to take the initiative and work with them. Try to find out why they're the way they are. Maybe they have just cause. Your slightly insecure boss could have been beaten down over the years by a bullying superior. Maybe all your boss lacks is confidence. You can help him become more emotionally secure by giving him positive feedback and encouragement.

A weak boss can sabotage you just as easily as an overly aggressive boss

---

Ask yourself if your boss has problems with any of these important areas. Give as many examples as you can.

- Working with his immediate superior (fearful of not pleasing his boss).
  Recent examples:

  _____

  _____

- Working with employees (fearful they're going to steal his job).
  Recent examples:

  _____

  _____

  _____

- Team management.
  Recent examples:

  _____

  _____

  _____

- Unfamiliar duties, new responsibilities.
  Recent examples:

  _____

  _____

  _____

- Learning from past mistakes.
  Recent examples:

  _____

  _____

  _____

- Willingness to take risks.
  Recent examples:

  _____

  _____

  _____

Helping your boss establish a proper balance between fear of failure and initiating progress is one of your greatest challenges.

The effective boss

The effective boss has his emotions under control, but is not afraid to display them when appropriate. He knows that without emotions, a corporate environment is dull, sterile and probably not competitive. Emotions can be used positively to motivate employees, build empathy and foster team spirit.

Effective bosses are willing and able to coordinate plans, programs and people with intelligence and understanding. They let employees know where they stand and guide the department to meet its goals and get the job done within the limitations of budget, staff or policy decisions.

To find out if you are working for an effective boss, ask yourself:

- Do his successes outnumber his mistakes?
- Does he handle failure realistically and move on to the next project with confidence?
- Does he avoid over-supervising his staff?
- Is he concerned about his employees' futures?
- Does his department make money?
- Does he expect the same high-level performance from himself that he expects from his employees?
- Does he recognize and reward employees who have performed well?
- Does he withhold rewards from employees who do *not* perform well?

Effective managers are good psychologists, using the varied emotional makeup of their employees to improve their department. They know when to support employees who lack confidence, when to bend rules for employees going through a crisis, when to give ambitious employees a chance to show what they can do. An effective boss prizes, above all, individual talents and abilities. He knows that a self-motivated staff will require less supervision, allowing him to explore and develop his own strengths.

Your boss's personal style

Your boss's personal style can say more about him than his list of goals. First, look at his style of communication. Is he formal or casual, preferring written memos to verbal messages or the reverse? A "paper person" likes to have information communicated first in readable form, followed by a personal talk. "People persons" are just the opposite, relying on meetings followed by detailed written reports.

It's important to understand that your boss's style of communication is based on how he processes information. So if your boss is paper-oriented, send him a memo, even if you hate adding to the departmental paper chase. And if he's people-oriented, don't hesitate to set up a short meeting to discuss new information.

Your boss's management style

Your boss's style of management may be the product of a self-image that thrives on flamboyance and fun. Does he see himself as an adventurer, charting the unknown seas of corporate enterprise? Does he give free rein to his imagination in tackling problems? Chances are, if he's innovative and gifted, he allows his employees the same kind of creative leeway. If this is the case, you couldn't ask for a better boss. But remember, the greater the leeway, the greater the potential risks. A daring and original leader, if allowed plenty of developmental latitude within the company, will recognize your inner resources and know how to make use of them.

A boss's style can often be shaped by his profession or previous career. Bosses who have served in the military, worked in law firms or government bureaucracies tend to be more formal, rigid and fond of doing things "by the book." A militaristic boss will emphasize the chain of command, reporting all matters to his immediate supervisor and following orders without much questioning.

A boss's management style can change—particularly when he, as an entrepreneur, has more personal freedom of expression. When small companies undergo rapid financial growth, your boss's style may also undergo a change—from a freewheeling small business owner to a more corporately correct CEO, ready to interact with presidents of other successful businesses.

Your boss's lifestyle

Evaluate, if you can, what your boss is like outside the office. You could be in for a big surprise. The ogre that has everybody trembling before a staff meeting could transform himself into an adoring parent at the sight of his 2-year-old.

It's always heartwarming to see a boss who's been cold and reserved at work exhibit warm feeling for his family and friends. You know that he has a life—a happy life—outside the office. The reasons for his hard-driven behavior at work become apparent. Your boss suddenly makes more sense to you in ways he never did before.

A boss's recreational interests say a lot about him. Does he prefer reading to tennis? Opera to country music? Fishing to race-car driving? And who does he share these enthusiasms with?

How your boss chooses to relax tells you about the other side of his personality. You might be surprised to learn that the stern disciplinarian you work for Monday through Friday is passionately fond of barbecue and, on the weekends, an amateur ornithologist.

Differences in personality can be wiped out if you discover you and your boss share a common interest, volunteer for the same community group or belong to the same church. Suddenly the boss you found so offensively loud and overbearing becomes more human. It helps to know that the person who demands those reports from you on Friday afternoon is the same one who coaches his daughter's softball team. It's easier for employees to work for bosses who, like them, have commitments to family, outside interests and community groups that expand and enrich their lives.

Ideas to build on

- Show your boss that you are willing to take the time to find out what he's all about. Learn about his goals and how to spot when they're in conflict.
- Carefully study how your boss uses both personal power and the power of his position. Use this knowledge to develop your relationship with him.
- Assess your boss's individual strengths and weaknesses, how he handles emotion, his perceived work style, personal interests and recreational activities.

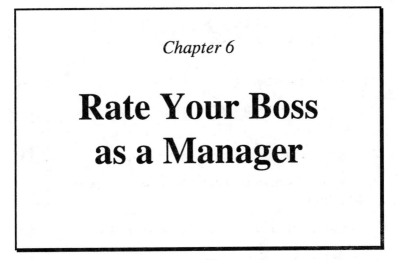

Chapter 6

Rate Your Boss as a Manager

To make the best use of the knowledge you are gaining about your boss, it is important that you evaluate her as objectively as possible. The profiling tool that follows was specifically designed for this purpose. It involves five basic areas for managerial assessment:

1. Management style.
2. Ability to plan.
3. Information and communication.
4. Time management.
5. Delegation.

For each area of management competence, determine if it is a definite strength your boss possesses, a definite weakness, or somewhere in between. Then give the appropriate score for your boss's performance.

Management style

Area of competence

Score

1. Is sensitive to the influence that her actions have on staff. ☐

2. Understands her reactions to my actions. ☐

3. Finds a balance between encouragement and pressure. ☐

4. Allows staff to express ideas and opinions. ☐

5. Is effective at motivating staff. ☐

6. Is able to resolve conflicts in a constructive way. ☐

7. Develops a spirit of teamwork among staff. ☐

8. Has a clear understanding of her role in the organization. ☐

9. Is tactful in disciplining a subordinate. ☐

10. Has a personal plan for self-improvement. ☐

Section Total ☐

Rating

10-9	**Definite strength**
8-7	**Moderately effective**
6-5	**Average performance**
4-3	**Rarely effective**
2-1	**Definite weakness**

Ability to plan

Area of competence   **Score**

1. Balances operations so that the pace is neither too routine nor too disruptive. ☐

2. Sufficiently analyzes the impact of particular changes on the future of the organization. ☐

3. Is sufficiently well-informed to pass judgment on the proposals that her subordinates make. ☐

4. Schedules meetings appropriately. ☐

5. Plans meetings in advance. ☐

6. Has a vision of the organization's direction. ☐

7. Has plans in written form to guide herself as well as others. ☐

8. Makes plans explicit in order to better guide the decisions of others in the organization. ☐

9. Is flexible enough to change, if necessary, to meet the changing needs of the organization. ☐

10. Schedules work to run smoothly. ☐

Section Total ☐

Rating
10-9	**Definite strength**
8-7	**Moderately effective**
6-5	**Average performance**
4-3	**Rarely effective**
2-1	**Definite weakness**

Information/communication

Area of competence   **Score**

1. Has good sources of information and methods for obtaining information. ☐

2. Has information organized so that it is easy to locate and use. ☐

3. Has other people do some scanning for her. ☐

4. Makes good use of contacts to get information. ☐

5. Balances collection of information with action. ☐

6. Gives staff needed information on time. ☐

7. Puts information in written form so subordinates are not at an informational disadvantage. ☐

8. Uses interoffice communications appropriately. ☐

9. Makes the most of meetings for which she is responsible. ☐

10. Spends enough time visiting other areas to obtain first-hand the results accomplished. ☐

Section Total ☐

Rating

10-9	**Definite strength**
8-7	**Moderately effective**
6-5	**Average performance**
4-3	**Rarely effective**
2-1	**Definite weakness**

Time management

Area of competence	Score

Area of competence **Score**

1. Has a time scheduling system. ❏

2. Avoids reacting to the pressure of the moment. ❏

3. Avoids concentrating on one function or type of problem just because it is interesting. ❏

4. Schedules particular kinds of work to take advantage of her energy/effectiveness levels. ❏

5. Controls interruptions of her work. ❏

6. Balances current, tangible activities with time for reflection and planning. ❏

7. Key priorities receive proper attention. ❏

8. Makes use of time-saving technology. ❏

9. Has priorities in mind most of the time. ❏

10. Has necessary information available at the right time to meet deadlines. ❏

Section Total ❏

Rating
10-9   **Definite strength**
8-7   **Moderately effective**
6-5   **Average performance**
4-3   **Rarely effective**
2-1   **Definite weakness**

Delegation

Area of competence   **Score**

1. Staff members understand objectives and know what is to be done, when and by whom. ☐

2. Knows which responsibilities to delegate. ☐

3. Encourages initiative in subordinates. ☐

4. Leaves final decision to staff often enough. ☐

5. Avoids doing staff's work. ☐

6. Shows genuine interest in staff's work. ☐

7. Is confident that staff can handle the work given to them. ☐

8. Gives staff guidance, training and authority they need to make decisions independently. ☐

9. Regularly assesses the quality of her work and that of staff. ☐

10. Uses delegation to help staff gain new skills and grow in the organization. ☐

Section Total ☐

Rating
10-9	**Definite strength**
8-7	**Moderately effective**
6-5	**Average performance**
4-3	**Rarely effective**
2-1	**Definite weakness**

Put your boss's score from each of the five sections into the appropriate boxes:

Management style ☐

Ability to plan ☐

Information and communication ☐

Time management ☐

Delegation ☐

Then determine, based on the following scoring grid, how high or low your boss scored in each section.

Rating
100-90	**Definite strength**
80-70	**Moderately effective**
60-50	**Average performance**
40-30	**Rarely effective**
20-10	**Definite weakness**

This should help you determine the areas in which your boss needs the most help and what you can do to be most helpful in those areas.

Begin by listing the areas with the lowest score. List under each of them specific actions you can take. For example, if your boss has a score of 45 for Information and communication, you could:

- Ask if you could be responsible for gathering data for reports that have been chronically late.
- Draft an agenda for the weekly staff meetings for her approval.

- Keep minutes of meetings and circulate them.
- Investigate the costs of providing fax machines for all district offices.

Strong boss or weak boss?

A quick way to evaluate your boss's management and leadership skills is to compare and contrast the traits of strong and weak bosses. Which is your boss?

Managerial role

Strong Boss
- Understands her role as a manager.
- Sees herself as a team leader.
- Accepts managerial responsibility.
- Tries to develop staff.

Weak Boss
- Can't distinguish between managerial and nonmanagerial work.
- Sees herself as "the boss."
- Avoids accountability.
- Is not concerned with employee development.

Duties and job knowledge

Strong Boss
- Always open to new things.
- Enjoys and understands the job.
- Can handle duties.

Weak Boss
- Has stopped learning new things.
- Hates job, doesn't understand it.
- Job has outgrown her.

Communications

Strong Boss
- Accessible.
- Initiates.
- Uses a variety of methods.

Weak Boss
- Inaccessible.
- Hides a lot.
- Uses only top-down method.

Leadership

Strong Boss
- Praises and rewards employees.
- Asks about and monitors employees' progress.
- Helps employees set goals.
- Fosters teamwork.

Weak Boss
- Seldom praises.
- Leaves employees alone.
- Not goal-oriented.
- Makes separate deals with individuals.
- Avoids conflict at all costs.

How to Manage Your Boss

Change

Strong Boss

- Seeks innovative methods.
- Receptive to new ideas.
- Expects quick change.
- Copes easily with change.

Weak Boss

- Maintains status quo.
- Discourages new ideas.
- Lets things happen slowly.
- Has trouble with new procedures.

Decision-making

Strong Boss

- Flexible.
- Participative.
- Open. Enjoys new challenges.

Weak Boss

- Rigid.
- Authoritative.
- Closed.
- Avoids challenges.

Ideas to build on

Even below-par bosses can become good bosses with the help of supportive employees. To develop a "big picture" of where you can start to assist your boss, ask yourself these questions:

- How can I convince my boss to include staff in decision-making?
- How can I help my boss overcome her fear of confronting employees—particularly when they're angry?
- How can I increase the frequency and quality of feedback she receives?
- Can I help my boss be a better team leader by bringing out the best in each of us?
- What support can I give my boss that will increase her visibility and effectiveness within this company?

The answers should help you develop strategies that will improve your boss's management and leadership abilities.

Most successful people attribute at least part of their style to one or more good bosses who made a lasting impression at some point in their career. Learn to value a good boss. If your boss needs some help to become *really* good, help her...and more often than not, you'll have a great relationship.

Chapter 7

What Are Your Boss's Needs?

All bosses need staff who will support them, keep them informed and, above all, understand their needs. But many bosses, like the rest of us, have never actually identified what their needs are. Fortunately, many are universal.

What every boss needs

Every boss needs staff who can be counted upon:

- To be trustworthy, dependable and loyal.
- To perform effectively.
- To relay vital information promptly.
- To protect his time.
- To be sensitive to pressures the boss is under.

Loyalty and dependability

Your boss needs to trust you just as you need to trust him. Being a trustworthy employee means being loyal to your boss and being dependable. Your boss wants an employee who will support his decisions, help him prevent mistakes, avoid political games, show up for work—and work!

Your trustworthiness is the solid foundation of your relationship with your boss. In exchange for your loyalty and trustworthiness, your boss should reward you by going to bat for you with upper-level management.

But if you're not loyal, beware. You may exhibit talent, brains and ambition, but if your boss feels he can't trust you, you're going nowhere within the organization.

To demonstrate your loyalty to your boss:

- Follow good work habits.
- Be punctual and stay focused.
- Do your job without complaining.
- Don't undermine your boss's efforts.

Perform effectively

Your boss is judged on how well *you* perform. So, accomplishment is the most important way to further your relationship with your boss.

The best bosses also expect their employees to be committed to improvement. If your boss sees you as someone who will do "whatever it takes," and is punctual, thorough and dependable, you will gain the credibility and leverage you need to succeed.

To show your boss that you are an effective performer:

- *Take the initiative.* Perform necessary tasks without being asked to do them. Be a "self-starter."
- *Solve problems.* Don't appear helpless when confronted with something new.

- *Use resources wisely.* Don't give the impression that more money will solve everything. It won't. Make use of the expertise or knowledge available in other departments (or outside your company) to get problems solved and work completed.
- *Don't complain.* Identify problems and bring possible solutions while there is still time to fix them. Explain the problem concisely; list your alternatives, and specifically explain the type of help you need and the steps you will follow.
- *Ask questions when you don't understand.* If you don't ask, you won't find out.

Relay vital information promptly

You can strengthen your boss's position by passing along vital information. You can also effectively sabotage him by not sharing something he needs to know. This applies particularly to what you learn in informal conversations, the rumor mill, shared group activities and other channels your boss may not be privy to.

Pass along what your boss needs to know, but avoid coming off as the office snitch. If your boss hears you spreading destructive gossip about co-workers or other bosses, he'll assume that you gossip in the same way about him.

To understand the difference between what your boss needs to know from mere idle gossip, ask yourself:

- Does this information affect my boss's position?
- Does this information affect the future of the company?
- Is this information something my boss needs to know about an employee, a project or relationship that could affect his decision?

Protect your boss's time

One of your boss's most valuable resources is his time. The higher a boss's position goes in the corporate structure, the more demands are made on his time. Since his effectiveness is measured by how well he accomplishes goals, it's up to you to help him plan his time carefully. Don't waste it in unnecessary conversations, meetings, reports or phone calls.

To protect your boss's time:

- Make sure the information you report is correct, clear, concise and as brief as possible.
- Help your boss turn time-consuming one-on-one meetings into more efficient group meetings.

Be sensitive to your boss's pressures

The first clue to a better understanding of the kind of pressure your boss is under is to take a look at *his* boss. Is your boss's boss undemanding, fair and loyal? Does he willingly extend support to your boss for his projects? Or is he a tough, aggressive line manager who views each department's contributions strictly in terms of profit and loss? Maybe there's a lot your boss would like to do for his employees but simply can't. He might be limited by budgetary considerations or a work style that differs widely from that of his own boss.

Once you've gauged the kind of pressure your boss deals with daily, you'll have a better feel for the ways in which you can meet his needs as a high-performing team player.

Companies undergo their greatest stress during periods of growth. So do bosses. If your company has recently undergone a merger, added new departments, changed its product line, or taken the opposite tack and begun to shed products and cut positions, take these steps to better meet the needs of your boss:

- Evaluate what kind of pressure the changes create for your boss.
- Keep abreast of market trends, competitive factors and technology changes that could have an impact, directly or indirectly, on your boss.

Your boss looks to you for results, not excuses. To be accountable, bring your boss recommendations, not more problems. Ask if you can study the situation and have a suggested solution in the morning. In addition, don't wait to be told what to do. Anticipate, analyze and propose action. And if you make a mistake, don't hide or try to blame it on something else. Take responsibility for it and move on.

Treat your boss with respect

Finally, never underestimate your boss, even if you're convinced he's totally incompetent. You just might be wrong—and that would be a terrible mistake to make.

Even if you overestimate your boss's abilities, you've made the right move by supporting him because you've gained an important ally. To get places within a company, almost everyone needs "help from above." That means from previous bosses who have liked, trusted and respected you. And what better way to move up than with a boss who's going places? You might as well make the trip first-class for both of you.

What your boss needs

While many needs are universal, your boss probably has some needs that are peculiar to your company or department. Finding out what those needs are can help you see him in a new light, and point to ways you can make yourself needed.

This may not be a simple process, though, because many bosses have never identified even to themselves what their needs are. They think in terms of jobs awaiting completion: stalled projects, piles of paperwork or frustrating "people problems." Your boss may need your help with his job and not even know it. Maybe you're just the person to compile those dull monthly reports or add some sprightly prose to his upcoming speech. The trick is in identifying these needs—and in getting him to acknowledge where he needs help.

Your boss may need your help with his job, and not even know it.

To begin identifying your boss's most intimate needs, answer these questions:

- What kind of stress is my boss under?
- What does he need from me?
- What frustrates him most?
- What is he doing that I could do as well or better?

Chapters 8 and 9 present specific ways to meet your boss's needs. You can use them to strengthen your relationship in ways that will amaze you.

Ideas to build on

To meet your boss's needs, you must first be trust-worthy and accountable, then protect his time and relay vital information. You must also observe the cardinal rule of all working relationships: never underestimate your boss. It's too expensive an error to make.

Only when you take the time to evaluate your boss's specific needs will you understand him well enough to be able to more effectively manage him. And there is a big bo-nus if you play your cards right. You will gain an important advocate...and you can never have too many allies.

Section III

Creating a Climate for Success

It's easy to manage your boss in a climate for success—a climate in which both of you are dedicated to the good of your department and company, can successfully set aside different working styles and petty concerns, and in which both of you understand that you are steadfastly on your boss's side.

In a climate of success, everybody wins. Your boss wins, because she knows that you are making her look as good as you can. You win, because you know that your efforts are being recognized and rewarded. And your company wins, because when you and your boss work together, the results you both want can be achieved.

Section III explains how to create a climate for success by creating a relationship that fits both of your key needs and styles.

These chapters will examine how to create a relationship in which you are effective. You'll learn how to help your boss succeed without losing your identity...how to meet your boss's needs without compromising your own...and how to communicate regularly and effectively.

Chapter 8

Your Success is My Success

Nobody wants to fail. Especially your boss. That's why the most successful bosses are committed to helping their employees succeed—and why the people who truly manage their bosses are effective in enabling them to succeed.

To help your boss succeed, you must:

- Demonstrate your commitment to your partnership, so your boss knows that you're in it together.
- Acknowledge that problems belong to both of you, and must be solved, not hidden.
- Help your boss avoid making mistakes.
- Work out your conflicts maturely.
- Bring your boss solutions, not problems.

Helping your boss succeed doesn't mean submitting to her every whim. Far from it. Success goes to those who can make the boss look good while still meeting their own needs. For example, if you excel at tasks that your boss prefers not to do, you win both ways. You capitalize on your strengths and, at the same time, take a load off her shoulders.

Demonstrate commitment to partnership

Your attitude is impossible to hide for long. If it varies widely from upbeat to doom and gloom, your boss will tend to classify you as unpredictable. From there, it's easy for her to soon have you in the box marked "unreliable."

Demonstrate your commitment to your partnership by eliminating attitude problems and being reliable, dependable and trustworthy. Work beyond the assignments you are given, and always surpass minimum requirements.

To really communicate a sense of partnership, always use the word "we" when referring to you and your boss. Avoid the "us/them" frame of mind that has so long plagued American business. You and your boss are partners even if your authority and status within the organization are not equal.

Acknowledge problems belong to both of you

When there's a hole in your boat, it doesn't matter whose side it's on. The boat will sink unless you fix it.

When a problem arises, propose answers and solutions to your boss. Don't wait for her to bring it up. Say, "We have a potential hole here. Let me recommend a way to get it plugged before it's a problem."

And don't waste any time blaming the problem on someone else. It's not just immature, it's dangerous. Which is more important? Fixing a problem and surviving, or insisting you're not at fault and going down with the ship?

In a situation like this, it's best to:

- Focus on the problem, not the people involved.
- Involve yourself in finding a solution.
- When you do these two things, it will always be difficult for people to think of you as a blamer.

(For help in presenting problems and other bad news to your boss, see the section in Chapter 10 called "Don't Shoot the Messenger!")

Help your boss avoid making mistakes

When you are committed and loyal to your boss, your first obligation is to help her avoid making mistakes. If you are truly loyal, you will never let your boss get into a situation where she becomes a laughing stock or is viewed as inept. It may be hard to work with a boss who is not qualified (and this may be common in family-owned businesses, where positions may be filled based on blood, not talent), but everyone must do it from time to time. Last but not least, if the situation goes on for more than a few months, change jobs!

To survive a stint with a boss who is not qualified:

1. Do your best to be supportive by doing your own job well.
2. Take on assignments that will provide you with skills you will need in the future.
3. Control your discontent and don't let it show. If you blow up, you may lose more than your temper.
4. Tactfully suggest workshops your boss could attend to learn more in areas of weakness.

5. Report on your progress and performance often. Keeping your boss current will remind her of what an asset you are and how much she needs you.

It's okay for you to make mistakes—so long as you learn from them. Most bosses won't mind, so long as they can see that the mistake has become a learning experience.

Work out conflicts with your boss

You and your boss won't always agree. Don't take your disagreements personally. When you disagree with your boss, take your *feelings* out of the conflict. Try to view the subject of your disagreement objectively. For example, if your boss says a report you prepared is biased by your personal opinions, ask "But what about facts one, two, and three?" If your boss falsely accuses you, ask for evidence. If you are tempted to say something in public that would insult her, shut up.

Remember, you and your boss are responsible for results, not lollipops and roses. It is unrealistic—even naive—to think that *any* two people can avoid conflict day-in and day-out.

By the way, don't confuse an insignificant difference in your personal styles for a yawning chasm in your relationship. Let your boss practice her personal style. If your boss is talkative, don't try to reform her. If she uses more words than necessary, that's perfectly all right. Don't aggravate things by projecting your own likes and dislikes onto your boss and rejecting her when she doesn't conform. And don't magnify those differences by dwelling on them. Be prepared to adapt. For example, if your boss is a schmoozer or touchy-feely and you're bottom-line oriented, you'll need to meet her at least halfway. Don't hit her with facts without warming up a little first.

Everyone, your boss included, deserves a chance to establish his or her own working "rhythm" and unfold his or her unique personality on the job. If you can't learn to live and work with people whose tastes, opinions and approaches to work differ from yours, you should become an entrepreneur and learn to count only on yourself. (You'll probably make more money if you do.)

Bring solutions, not problems

As problems arise, don't ignore them—resolve them. Volunteer to investigate sticky situations. Study, research and document, then stick your neck out and suggest what should be done. That's what accountability means. That's what makes you stand out in the crowd.

For example, when your boss is facing an unexpected problem that falls a little outside her area of expertise or comes on top of a critical deadline, offer to take over the job. Say, "Let me work on that tonight and I'll have a recommendation for you in the morning."

Ideas to build on

Helping your boss succeed doesn't mean that you need to lose your own identity. In days gone by, people got ahead by following the company line. But today, advancement is more likely if you have the courage and conviction to say what you think is right, and show your boss why.

Chapter 9

Specific Strategies for Success

The more your boss needs you, the stronger your position and the brighter your prospects. By ferreting out and meeting your boss's unique needs, you will *make yourself essential*—an enviable position for anyone in these uncertain economic times.

To make yourself essential:

- Help your boss anticipate problems.
- Quickly respond to his requests.
- Find out what your boss needs to know and get this information for him.
- Provide as much information as you can so your boss can make good decisions.
- Help your boss prepare for meetings.
- Save your boss time by simplifying tough issues.
- Monitor and eliminate irrelevant contacts (phone calls, interruptions, junk mail) that take up your boss's time.

- Volunteer to deal with difficult people.
- Screen out incompetent advisers.
- Offer honest, constructive criticism.
- Keep good records (notes of meetings, summaries of reports).

Your boss's unmet work needs

Use your answers to the questions in Chapter 7 to draw up a list of your boss's unmet work needs. For example, your boss may be desperate for help with some projects that are dangerously behind deadline. Or your boss may have some weaknesses—technical knowledge or attention to detail, for example—where your strengths can bail him out.

Helping your boss catch up

Your boss's work may not be part of your responsibilities—but if you can pitch in when he needs help, you'll surely gain favor. This is never more true than when vital work starts to run behind schedule or is neglected altogether.

When you offer to help your boss out with some of his work, be careful how you approach him. Depending on his level of self-confidence or how much he trusts you, your boss might interpret your action as an attempt to seize some of his power.

One way to meet your boss's needs in this situation is to help him get a grip on incoming paperwork. Especially if you excel at written communication and your boss does not, you could offer to summarize longer reports and memos and tell him about shorter ones.

Offer your strengths and skills

You were hired for your unique strengths and talents—qualities your boss thought could help his department succeed. Use your talents to go beyond your job description, especially if your boss struggles with tasks that are your strong suit. See if you can help your boss meet his work needs in any of the following ways:

If you have strong writing and communications skills:

1. Understand the core of what he wants to communicate, then write his longer memos and reports. He can then edit and give final approval.
2. Ghost-write his speeches and prepare audio-visuals for presentations.
3. Proofread, edit and see that major bases are covered in interdepartmental communication he authors.

When you have strong organizational skills:

1. Ask him to share his schedule with you so you can make appointments when he's busy elsewhere. Confirm all appointments and changes with him at the end of the day.
2. Introduce a new filing method or keep duplicate files of his work where you both have easy access to relevant projects.
3. Convince him to restructure meetings so time is used more effectively. For instance, combine group meetings instead of holding numerous individual ones.

When you have strong computer skills:

1. Volunteer to be the liaison between your department and your company's computer systems people. When technical problems arise, spare your boss the headache and get them solved.

2. Offer to teach your boss the basics of using your department's equipment. Show him how to send and receive an E-mail message, or open and save a document.

3. Surprise your boss with the fact that you have mastered a new skill on your own time and can now prepare flow charts using the latest software in your field.

Approaching your boss about unmet needs

No boss likes to be reminded of areas in which he is weak. That's why your effectiveness is determined by your approach. If he's open, enthusiastic and the two of you share a successful track record based on mutual trust and past accomplishments, you can be fairly open in your approach. To be safe, keep these guidelines in mind:

- Choose a time that's good for your boss—when he's not distracted, depressed by bad news or in the midst of planning for another meeting.

- Begin by complimenting him on something he does well. *"Congratulations on the new contract you negotiated. No one else in this company could have handled it so well."*

- Remain upbeat. Think of positive ways to express the help you're offering and why you're offering it.

Stress the benefits you'll each receive. *"I thought this would be good for both of us. Preparing the monthly report would be a good learning experience for me and at the same time would free you to concentrate on more important projects that coincide with the report's monthly deadline."*

- Be open to his suggestions. If your boss agrees to turn over some of his work to you, he'll probably want to experiment on a project-by-project basis.
- Be discreet. Let your boss know you'll take on this extra assignment in confidence without advertising it to co-workers.
- Provide closure without pressure. If he agrees to think about your offer, close by giving him feedback and proposing a deadline for a decision: *"You will be ready, then, to let me know your decision by next Wednesday?"* If he accepts your offer, but isn't definite, close by saying, *"Then you'll get the report data to me by next Wednesday and I'll give you a first draft by Friday?"*

When your relationship with your boss is less open, you may have to approach him more subtly. When he sees that you're not only hardworking and dependable but you also have skills he lacks, he'll eventually find a way to ask you for help, usually by "offering you a chance to prove yourself." In this case, accept graciously and let him think it was his idea.

Here are some ways you can indirectly advertise your skills to help your boss with his work needs:

- Offer your services on a specific project to a lateral boss with similar needs to your boss. (But get your boss's approval first!)

- Ask your boss to send you to a seminar in one of the areas you think you could be of help—time management or business communications, for example.

- After a positive review, tell your boss you'd like more responsibility. Be specific. List what you can do. Can he think of new ways to use your strengths?

And finally, be sure to distinguish between helping your boss meet his needs and becoming the unacknowledged "power behind the throne" who writes his speeches, prepares his annual reports and compiles the agendas for his meetings—all without adequate recognition or compensation. If your boss begins thinking of you as a blindly loyal staff member to whom he can entrust more and more work without recognizing and rewarding you, then it's time to update your resume, flap your wings and fly away.

Meeting your boss's emotional needs

Some bosses need to know they're liked by employees. Others don't seem to care what anyone thinks. Maybe your boss is generous and fair but needs to see himself as a family patriarch rather then as a departmental manager. No matter. You can help him be better by understanding his emotional needs and—when they're legitimate—meeting them.

Let's first identify some common emotional needs bosses have. See which ones fit your situation.

1. Positive feedback. Everyone needs to hear when they're doing a good job—even bosses. Give your boss a pat on the back now and then, particularly when he's distinguished himself by meeting difficult deadlines, winning awards or promotions. Your

positive feedback can mean a lot to your boss when he's going through a difficult time. Single out one of his better qualities—his leadership, his fairness, his sincerity—and let him know he's appreciated. Tell him you enjoy playing on his team.

2. Loyalty. You can show your loyalty to your boss by demonstrating good work habits—being punctual and focused—and by carrying out orders without undue complaining or questioning. Reserve criticism for one-on-one meetings. Bosses need loyal, trustworthy employees. In turn, he should reward you by going to bat for you with upper-level management.

3. Respect. No matter how laid-back or fun-loving a boss you have, he still needs your respect. Your boss is never more vulnerable than in front of his boss or upper-level management. If you see that your boss has switched gears into a more structured, formal approach, do him a favor and follow suit. Don't persist in addressing him informally or casually dropping by his office.

4. To be liked. Few if any humans prefer isolation. Your boss is no exception. Identify his most admirable characteristic and commend him for it.

5. Control. People cast in leadership positions do not want to feel dependent. They want to exert strong influence and control. Help them by giving them information they need *before* they need it.

By figuring out what your boss needs emotionally, you'll be fulfilling a subtle requirement that is never mentioned in a job description. When you meet your boss's emotional needs, he'll rely on you, trust you, confide in you more than he would a more highly skilled but less empathetic co-worker.

Unreasonable emotional needs

Occasionally, bosses make excessive emotional demands on their employees and co-workers. Their actions are prompted by unresolved emotional needs that seem to come from a bottomless pit of insecurity and low self-esteem. Bosses who use you as an emotional crutch, are overly controlling, or are not open to suggestions or criticism may require careful handling. Chapter 14 outlines strategies for succeeding with many such specimens.

Unreasonable control is stifling. If your boss restricts your actions to "his way," explain how this limits your ability to perform effectively. Detail the consequences.

If your boss is too chummy, back away without a confrontation. Don't accept invitations to a lot of social situations if you know you will be uncomfortable.

What happens when your boss's emotional needs infringe upon your sense of what's appropriate or inappropriate?

When your boss's behavior goes beyond obnoxious and becomes dangerous or illegal (threats, sexual harassment, contract violation, etc.), you need to act swiftly and firmly. Here again you will find help in Chapter 15.

Work style conflicts

Conflicts with bosses often arise from different styles of working. Consider yourself lucky if your work style meshes smoothly with that of your boss. Here are some typical examples of conflicting work styles:

Employee needs:
- To work autonomously.
- Spontaneous feedback/strokes.
- To have freedom to be creative.

Boss needs:
- To be constantly involved and continuously supervise employees' work.
- To remain aloof, protect his privacy. Views spontaneity as a "weak" style of management.
- To control all aspects of work assignments.

In each of these examples, employee-boss needs differ radically. As an employee, you certainly have met successful management practitioners who believe that bosses must be responsive to their employees' needs. Here are some steps you can follow to ensure that mutual expectations are met without either party feeling unduly compromised:

1. Evaluate how deeply ingrained your boss's work style is. How long has he held his position? Has he ever worked differently?
2. Do other employees feel the same way you do? A boss may be more likely to listen to five employees instead of one about the need for change.
3. Make sure you and your boss define mutual expectations. Be specific about what you need to do to be more productive.
4. Be willing to compromise.

Even if you're successful at only negotiating some small change in your boss's work style—say, initiating weekly staff meetings with an aloof boss—you've won a huge battle. It means your boss is willing to listen to what you have to say and make changes. Thank him for his cooperation and begin to build a track record with him. That way, the next time a conflict of work styles arises, he'll know that making a change is worth the trouble.

Ideas to build on

Meeting your boss's needs can help you create a fruitful, longlasting relationship with your boss. To make yourself indispensable, search for your boss's unique, unmet needs, and take action to meet them.

Your priorities and your boss's priorities will not always match. When your needs and your boss's needs are in conflict, it's best to resolve problems by getting feedback on your mutual expectations. Be clear about the changes you need from your boss to do a better job—then, when he accommodates your request, do your best to prove that both of you are right.

Chapter 10

Building Better Communication with Your Boss

People are the only creatures who can talk themselves into trouble. Fortunately, they can also communicate their way out of it!

This ability to communicate is a vital factor in your success. It lets you persuade, clarify a confusing situation, send and receive important information, and demonstrate sincere interest in your boss and others around you. It also enables you to bring your accomplishments to the foreground.

Maintaining open communication lines between you and your boss can pay dividends. Open lines will help you:

- Maintain awareness of how your boss feels and thinks.
- Respond intelligently to criticism on actions you have taken.
- Handle questions fully.

- Explain clearly the reasons behind a decision you made.
- Contribute significantly to the content of meetings.

It isn't just emergency situations that require communication skills. Good communication is key to managing your boss—because unless you communicate, you simply won't have a relationship to manage.

Unless you communicate, you simply won't have a relationship to manage.

Communication is more than just talk. This chapter will give you pointers on communicating effectively with your boss face to face and in writing. It will also help you diagnose communication patterns gone sour, and restore them to health.

No matter how positive your relationship with your boss, you can benefit from learning how to communicate more effectively, more efficiently and more clearly.

Talking with—and listening to—your boss

Every conversation with your boss is important, whether you chat near the soda machine or sit down together for a lengthy discussion.

Consider how you actually speak to your boss. Are you quick to put your thoughts into words, or do you take time to formulate your ideas? Hesitancy on your part can be construed as lack of knowledge, whereas responding too quickly can make you seem impulsive or abrupt and rude.

Whether you are meeting formally or informally, follow these specific suggestions:

1. Time your speech patterns by recording a conversation you might have with your boss. Do you need to slow down or speed up?
2. If you're having trouble verbalizing, give your boss some feedback: "Bear with me, I'm finding the best way to phrase this."
3. If you're too quick, give yourself some extra time to respond; count five beats before talking.
4. Ask a co-worker who is a good friend to critique how you communicate with your boss.

Above all, *think* before you speak, and practice putting your thoughts into words. It is important to say what is really on your mind!

When the subject of your discussion requires a formal meeting, make an appointment to see your boss. One-to-one meetings with bosses are the most direct and focused type of communication. These guidelines will be helpful:

- Determine what the objective of the meeting is.
- Determine if your boss is a good candidate for a meeting.
- Organize your thoughts.
- Know exactly what you want to talk about.
- Choose the time and place for the meeting wisely.

Defining the problem and determining your objectives are two separate tasks. Before asking for a meeting with your boss, you need to clearly define the problem or issues you want to discuss. If your boss absorbs information better by reading, then prepare an outline or written summary. If your boss prefers to hear information, organize and summarize the situation in a succinct but thorough verbal response. When you are in the meeting be sure to:

- Speak and listen calmly and objectively.
- Describe the objective of your meeting concisely.
- Summarize key points that pertain to the discussion.
- Present your conclusion, proposed solution or alternative actions that can be taken.
- Listen carefully to your boss's response. Does she indicate she understood you? If not, rephrase and summarize to correct any misconceptions.
- When responding to your boss's concerns or objections, restate the specific concern, and then explain your position.
- Seek common ground—points on which you both agree.
- Seek solutions or an action plan that is mutually acceptable.
- Summarize any decisions that are made. Be sure they are understood by both of you.

To communicate effectively to your boss and gain her cooperation:

- Share information while it is still fresh.
- Focus your attention on what the topic means personally to your boss.
- Be generous in recognizing your boss's viewpoint.
- Seek clarification with phrases such as "Are you comfortable with that?" "What is your reaction?"

When it's your turn to listen:

- Focus on your boss and show an interest in what she is saying.
- Refrain from interrupting.
- Listen carefully to make sure your boss is properly interpreting your words.

When a meeting may not be productive

Few bosses handle meetings well. Defensive or angry bosses may try all sorts of postponing, stalling and interrupting tactics. Ask yourself these questions to determine if a meeting with your boss is likely to be productive:

- *Can your boss take criticism?* Good bosses want honest feedback from their employees. Realize that there are appropriate times and places to give your boss constructive criticism. Rule number one is never criticize your boss in front of others. No matter how well-intended, it can embarrass her; it can make you look tactless and blundering.
- *Is your boss a good problem-solver?* No matter how buried she is in other projects, a good boss will jump right on a problem before it mushrooms into a colossal crisis.
- *Is your boss decisive? Not afraid to make a decision?*
- *Does your boss attack problems or hope they'll go away?*
- *Does your boss claim she lacks the authority to do anything about it?*
- *Is your boss vindictive?* Does she seem open and accepting of what you're telling her, but start

sharpening her knives the moment you're out of the office? If you're not sure, ask around. See if there are any co-workers who, after registering complaints or criticism, quit, were fired or transferred to other departments.

- *Is your boss honest and caring?* Your boss shouldn't betray what you've said in confidence to hurt others or hurt you. She shouldn't use the intimacy of the meeting to lull you into a position of false trust, trying to get you to reveal things you may regret later. If your boss is caring, you'll know it. Caring can't be faked.

- *Is your boss objective?* Can she make tough decisions that are for the good of the company? Can she be critical of her own ideas and projects?

- *Is your boss a good listener?* Does she make eye contact, ask questions and reiterate your main points? Or does she try to do two things at once, play with objects on her desk, stare out the window or frequently interrupt you?

You might get your boss to be a better listener by suggesting you reschedule the meeting or asking her for direct feedback on what you've said, so as to get her directly involved.

Setting up a meeting

You can propose the idea of a meeting face-to-face, in writing, or via phone, E-mail or fax. Don't ask for a meeting when:

- The boss is visibly upset.
- She's just come from a difficult meeting with her boss.

- She first arrives in the office.
- She is about to leave the office.
- She's in the middle of an important project, preparing for a meeting or presentation or rushing to meet a deadline.

Tell your boss the purpose of the meeting. Don't make it a mystery. While your real objective may be to open up communication, this alone is not a good reason. Have a purpose and be as specific as possible.

If your boss starts waffling about a convenient time, don't take "later" for an answer. Keep confronting her (politely!) until she agrees to a definite date and time. Offer to check with her assistant to find a convenient time to schedule. Suggest some alternative times, three or so, for her to choose from.

How to prepare for your meeting

If your purpose is to define mutual expectations, write a memo to give your boss before the meeting, detailing the areas you'd like clarified. Stay specific. Cite particular instances and dates, such as late shipments in March, inaccuracies in July sales reports, or the $40,000 budget shortfall on new software for claims processing. Ask if her list is the same as yours.

Remember, your boss doesn't have a lot of time to spend reading. If you've presented her with a 20-page memo before the meeting, she may lose all interest in accommodating your requests because of the mountains of paperwork you generate. Stick to the facts. Don't exaggerate. And keep an objective but cooperative tone.

How to conduct a meeting

During any introductory small talk and throughout the meeting, be aware of the body language each participant projects. It can tell you a lot more than the actual words being spoken.

Check for openness and genuine interest. Remember, this applies as much to you as to your boss. Don't slouch in the chair, arms folded, turned away from your boss. Sit up straight, place your feet on the floor and assume an assertive, responsive expression—even if you're feeling a little intimidated.

Watch for body language with a positive meaning:

- Open, relaxed position facing each other squarely.
- Arms at sides or hands folded casually in lap.
- Good eye contact.
- Pleasant, attentive facial expression.
- Good posture.

If your boss exhibits some or all of these traits, it means you're coming through loud and clear, and she's receiving the information positively.

You should also watch for body language with a more negative interpretation:

- Crossed arms.
- Body in a sideways position.
- Frowning or stone-faced expression.
- Frequently looking at watch.
- Tapping toe.
- Drumming fingers.

If you see any of these traits, stop—unless your objective is to make your boss even more uncomfortable. One way to reduce negative body language is to engage your boss directly in the exchange of information. You can ask her for feedback by saying, "How do you feel about these problems?" This way you can address any misunderstandings immediately.

Even when it's your boss's turn to do the talking, you still have to be watchful and aware—not only of what she's saying, but of the kind of unspoken information she's giving you.

In stressful situations, it's tempting to stop paying attention when the other party is speaking and think of what you're going to say next. By not "tracking" we lose part of what the other person is saying. It's easy for them to "read" our impatience to speak. Be sure when your boss is talking that you give her constant feedback, both verbal and non-verbal by:

- Giving direct attention: assume straight posture, make eye contact, nod in agreement when appropriate.
- Asking questions when your boss pauses for feedback.
- Encouraging your boss by inviting response: *"I'm really interested in hearing your reaction to this ..."*
- Restating what your boss has said to let her know you understand.

Asking thought-provoking questions may sound difficult, especially when you're already nervous about presenting your end of the discussion persuasively. But if you learn to listen closely, you'll pick up on key points. In fact, your boss will be impressed with your ability to quickly grasp her points.

Repeating what your boss has said allows you to paraphrase her argument. You can begin by summarizing essential points, *"You're saying that we must first cut spending in the department, and that our other needs will have to wait."*

To emphasize your partnership and prevent defensiveness, avoid emotionally loaded language like *"You really screwed up when you..."* By all means, be candid. But try to eliminate judgmental words from your verbal communication. Words like should, ought, good and bad only prompt anger and defensiveness.

Always make it clear you're communicating your observations, not absolute truth. Avoid sweeping generalizations such as, *"Bill always makes mistakes"* or *"Sue never completes a job on time."* Avoid using the words "always" and "never." Stick to the facts. If you can't back up your beliefs with evidence, back off.

Ending a meeting

A meeting usually ends with the two parties reaching a mutual agreement. When it's you and your boss, a good ending is a performance agreement that satisfies the needs of both parties. Your meeting purpose and performance agreement could look like this:

Purpose of Meeting
For my boss to be more specific about what kind of feedback she needs from me and at what times.

Performance Agreement
My boss and I agree to meet once a week to discuss my reports outlining the accomplishments of my staff. At the end of each month we will review goals for the next month.

Remember to make your performance agreement as specific and concise as possible. No one likes to leave a meeting with a performance agreement that is too general to be measured against. For instance, stay away from generalities like "schedule more meetings with boss."

When it's time for you to shake hands and come out of the office smiling, make sure you end the meeting in a spirit of cooperation. Thank your boss for her time. She has done you a favor, even if it's going to work to her benefit, too.

How to follow up a meeting

For the most important meetings, write your boss a memo detailing key points and decisions that were reached. You might want to end with, *"If this is not your understanding of what transpired, please let me know."* That way, should there be any future discussion of you not keeping up your end of the performance agreement, you have your understanding of the meeting's results in writing.

Arrange for a follow-up meeting in the near future to see how you both are dealing with the changes you've introduced. Remember, improving your communication with your boss doesn't come from a single meeting, but from a series of fine tunings and adjustments until you have a process that works for both of you.

Don't shoot the messenger!

Candor is important in any organization. While no one really likes to be the bearer of bad news, it must be passed along. Problems that are covered up or ignored will fester until they burst into full-blown monsters. Far better to bite the bullet and tell your boss about a crack in the dike than to wait and deliver the news that the dam has broken.

Delivering bad news *is* risky. Some messengers are fired on the spot. But if you have built a solid relationship, the risk will diminish.

First, take steps to help your boss see you as a source of all kinds of news, not just bad. In your regular contacts, pass along a variety of vital information, as well as items from the grapevine, or even a good joke. Avoid being the sort of person who only consults the boss when a problem arises. If all of your contacts are pleas for help or news of disaster, your boss will see you as a problem-starter, not a problem-solver.

Observe how your boss reacts to bad news from others, and use that information to determine the best approach to delivering your message. A task-oriented boss may want to hear the news directly. Someone with a more analytical bent may want the background first, the news last. In some situations, you might want reassurance first. When you know how your boss reacts, you can prepare a contingency plan.

When it's your turn to share bad news:

- Don't hide behind a memo. Plan to deliver the news in person as soon as possible, so you can straighten out misperceptions and focus the conversation on solutions.

- Find out as much as you can about the situation before your report it.

- If it's your fault, admit it up front.

- If it's your boss's fault, try to depersonalize the news. Instead of saying "*Your* plan is not working" say "*The* plan is not working."

- If it's someone else's fault entirely, use the meeting to strategize how to cut your losses.
- Lay out the facts, lay out the alternatives and tell which one you recommend and why.
- Include lots of quotes from your sources, so your boss knows you are passing along valid information.

If the bad news raises your boss's hackles, let her vent her feelings. Wait until she's finished before examining alternatives and planning a course of action. When the meeting is over and a remedy is underway, keep your boss posted on the status of the solution.

The rules of writing a memo

Use memos and reports to communicate to others— including your boss—what a professional you are. Don't blame clerical errors on your secretary! You're ultimately responsible for anything that goes out with your name on it.

- Make sure content is well-organized and structured correctly and that your ideas are communicated clearly.
- Proofread and correct any grammar, spelling or punctuation errors.
- Never communicate through memos when you're angry.
- Never communicate through memos information you wouldn't want others to see. A memo marked "confidential and private" may end up in the wrong hands, or be used to hurt you by an unscrupulous boss.

Use memos to:

- Document occurrences and facts.
- Assure accuracy of records.
- State an agreement or confirm one.
- Remind or refresh memories.

Solving communication problems

Sometimes communication between you and your boss goes awry. You may not be able to pinpoint what's wrong, but you sense that your boss is not giving you proper guidance to get the job done or that you aren't communicating well.

Example 1

You tell all your friends what a great boss you have. It's almost like working for an older sister. You can pop into her office any time to ask her questions or just shoot the breeze. She often drops by your cubicle to tell you about her latest date, then inquires as she's ready to leave, "Hey, any problems with that last project I gave you?" Actually, you do have a few problems, but you hate to bring them up and ruin the great time the two of you are having.

In this example, your boss has encouraged you to think of her as a "pal." There is nothing wrong with a boss having an open-door policy, but when traffic is not controlled and employees rush in with fires to be put out, office gossip or questions they could have easily answered themselves, a manager's precious time vanishes. Likewise, a boss who drops by an employee's cubicle to discuss personal issues while ignoring the project at hand is acting irresponsibly and unprofessionally.

Your boss can't figure out why her employee is so under-motivated and unable to meet deadlines—why productivity and work quality are poor. After all, the boss gives up precious time to listen to her staff whenever they want to talk.

You finally realize that you cannot get your work done because of poor supervision and interrupted work habits. When the ax falls, it will be on your head, not your boss's.

Both of you are wasting each other's time in these friendly chats. First, change your behavior—greatly reduce the amount of time you initiate nonwork chatting with your boss. If you are interrupted by your boss who begins talking about her personal life, suggest that you postpone your conversation until lunch or chat after work. Finally, you must discuss any work-related problems you have with your boss as soon as they arise. If it becomes apparent your boss wants to cultivate a friendship, then suggest that you get together outside the office. Friends who work together need to be able to separate their professional relationship and their friendship.

Example 2

You work for a guy you really respect. Everyone in the company agrees that he's not only good, he's brilliant at what he does. He's published articles. He's even been appointed by the mayor to serve on special committees. You realize this boss is on his way up. You've asked him for more responsibility and he gives you a difficult project to accomplish within a tight deadline. You've tried a few times to get him to help you with some problems you are having, and he just brushes you off. You feel like you must be the most incompetent assistant he's ever had.

Here, your boss is clearly not used to working within an office hierarchy, or at least isn't skilled at managing employees. At first, the picture looked rosy to both you and your boss. You're both bright, ambitious people who value a certain degree of autonomy. However, when your boss gave you more responsibility, he obviously didn't pass along much training or helpful information.

Your boss is used to dealing with people who have the experience to complete a project without help. You asked for a more interesting project, and he gave you one. Now he perceives you as a nuisance, always pestering him with trivial questions. With all his other responsibilities, he really doesn't have the time or inclination to nurse you along.

The deadline is closing in. If the project isn't done right, you will look twice as incompetent because you asked for additional work. The relationship with your boss seems to be disintegrating rapidly. You really need help, and you don't even know how to talk to the guy anymore.

You need to first define the nature of the problem you face and determine what it will take to solve it. Information? Specialized skills or expertise? Money? Once the problem and the resources needed to complete the project are identified, you need to determine if anyone else can help you. If so, you can seek help from others. If not, you should document the nature of the problem and the solution in a memo to your boss.

The key is to communicate concisely. Most bosses hate having to answer a series of unrelated questions or deal with a problem in a piecemeal fashion. Then you should be assertive about getting a response. If your boss is always in the office at 7:30 a.m. or on weekends, grab a few minutes of his time then. If you find him unresponsive, emphasize the importance of this project, your commitment to it and how you would hate for any problems to arise that could prove to be an embarrassment to either of you.

Example 3

The woman who was newly hired to manage your department has never worked in sales before. Her background is in accounting. You can see she's making some very basic mistakes. In a staff meeting, when she asks for questions or suggestions, you offer a few helpful hints on how she should improve. Although she tries not to show it, you can tell she's irritated. She has ignored you for the past week now, and you don't know what you did wrong.

You see ways to help your new department head be a better manager, but you choose the wrong way to criticize her: in a staff meeting. The relationship has been damaged by your tactlessness and her defensiveness.

You chose the most damaging time to offer suggestions on how to perform better. She concludes that either you are ignorant of office protocol or you're consciously undermining her. You believe you were honestly trying to help. Maybe the staff meeting wasn't the best place to offer advice, but you feel she asked for such advice when she opened the discussion for suggestions.

Ask for a few minutes of your boss's time to talk. At that time, apologize for embarrassing her in front of the staff. Acknowledge your lack of sensitivity and your appreciation for her feelings as a newcomer. Indicate that even though the two of you got off on the wrong foot, you want to do whatever you can to support your boss. It is very unlikely that you can communicate effectively until the air has been cleared regarding this incident.

When communication breaks down, the fragile relationship between boss and employee can be irreparably damaged. The fault is rarely just one person's. As in marriages that falter, both partners in a working relationship contribute their share to the communication problem. If your boss is a good manager, he'll understand his responsibilities and take the initiative to prevent festering. When your boss won't attempt to solve a communication problem, however, it's in your best interest to take charge and start looking for solutions.

Ideas to build on

At work, you will be better off if you learn the skills that will enable you to carry 60 percent of the communication load—leaving your boss responsible for only 40 percent. Once you accept that ratio, you will have fewer disappointments and many more successes.

- Use regular meetings to build good rapport with your boss and forge a relationship that can support you when it's your turn to deliver bad news.
- Prepare for meetings with your boss by clearly identifying your purpose, the projected outcome and what you want to communicate.
- Ask for an appointment at an appropriate time and prepare a memo of what you plan to cover.
- During the meeting, pay attention to the nonverbal feedback you're getting from and giving to your boss.
- Stay focused and responsive during the meeting.
- Afterwards, be sure to thank your boss for his time.
- Follow up with any necessary documentation such as summaries or performance agreements.

Section IV

Maintain Your Relationship With Your Boss

It's important to maintain your relationship with your boss by communicating your feelings and expectations, and by monitoring carefully for signs of problems.

In this section, you'll learn how to tell when the relationship is working and what to do when it isn't.

Chapter 11

How You'll Know
It's Working

You'll know your relationship with your boss is working when you:

- Respect your boss, and are respected by him.
- Trust your boss, and are trusted by him.
- Know that your loyalty is mutual and both of you are looking out for each other's best interests.
- Feel confident about your future.

Throughout every page of this book, I've tried to provide you with tools you can use to create a mutually beneficial relationship. Here are five final key areas that you must be prepared to work on:

- Sharpen your competitive edge.
- Take risks.
- Help your boss manage change.
- Practice candor.
- Monitor and evaluate your performance.

Sharpen your competitive edge

The best mindset on which to build a positive relationship with your boss is to believe that your competitive edge is *you*. You must decide how to spend your time, effort and energy. You need to pinpoint what you need to learn—and learn it. When you allow yourself to learn from your mistakes and avoid blaming anyone else for them, you can truly sharpen your skills and abilities to create a competitive edge.

The Competitive Edge Profile, which follows on the next page, can help you assess your strengths and point out areas in which you need work.

As you think about the abilities you need to polish or acquire, look beyond obvious technical skills. While these are important, the skills you need to move up the hierarchy are less tangible skills—such as the ability to influence, the ability to persuade and the ability to lead. For example, you might want to select from the following as skills that you want to work on:

- Emotional maturity.
- Stamina.
- Decision-making ability.
- Communications skills.
- Perseverance.
- Self-discipline.
- Listening without interrupting.
- Asking good questions.
- Simplifying methods.
- Initiating actions without prompting.
- Flexibility.

Competitive Edge Profile

1. What do you do best now? List your skills.

_____

_____

_____

_____

_____

2. What is preventing you from achieving your career objectives?

_____

_____

_____

_____

3. Where are you most vulnerable? Why?

_____

_____

_____

_____

_____

Competitive Edge Profile

4. In priority order, what are your three greatest needs right now? Health? Relationships? Skills? Career progress?

   1. _____

   2. _____

   3. _____

5. Where do you want to be in three years?

   1. _____
      _____

   2. _____
      _____

   3. _____
      _____

Based on your answers, identify changes you need to make to sharpen your competitive edge. Follow this format.

Change required: _____
_____
_____

Expected result: _____
_____

By when: _____

Help needed, if any: _____
_____
_____

Competitive Edge Profile

Change required: _____

_____

_____

Expected result: _____

_____

_____

_____

By when: _____

Help needed, if any: _____

_____

_____

Change required: _____

_____

_____

Expected result: _____

_____

_____

_____

By when: _____

Help needed, if any: _____

_____

_____

Competitive Edge Profile

Change required: _____

_____

_____

Expected result: _____

_____

_____

_____

By when: _____

Help needed, if any: _____

_____

_____

Change required: _____

_____

_____

Expected result: _____

_____

_____

_____

By when: _____

Help needed, if any: _____

_____

_____

Competitive Edge Profile

Identify your strengths that will enable you to sharpen your competitive edge:

Strength: _____

_____

Recent evidence/proof: _____

_____

_____

Confirmed by whom and when: _____

_____

_____

Strength: _____

_____

Recent evidence/proof: _____

_____

_____

Confirmed by whom and when: _____

_____

_____

Strength: _____

_____

Recent evidence/proof: _____

_____

_____

Confirmed by whom and when: _____

_____

Competitive Edge Profile

List your three career objectives, and rate how close you are to achieving them, from 1 (low) to 10 (high). Then determine how much you can improve your rating in the next year. Can you move from 5 to 7? from 2 to 5? from 6 to 9?

Career objective #1:_____

_____

Career objective #2:_____

_____

Career objective #3:_____

_____

Answer these questions to determine the steps you should take in order to raise your score:

Career objective #1
What should you do first to be more competitive?

_____

_____

_____

When can you take this first step?

_____

_____

_____

Who can help you make it?

_____

_____

Competitive Edge Profile

Career objective #2
What should you do first to be more competitive?

_____

_____

When can you take this first step?

_____

_____

Who can help you make it?

_____

Career objective #3
What should you do first to be more competitive?

_____

_____

When can you take this first step?

_____

_____

Who can help you make it?

_____

_____

- Adjusting to new situations.
- Gatherings facts.
- Prioritizing.
- Ability to sustain effort on less praise.

None of these changes will take place unless you make them happen. Sharpening your competitive edge is up to you!

Take risks

When you take risks, you stand out. And that's something your organization—and your boss—may value. The person who doesn't share opinions and never breaks out of "group think" risks being overlooked for new opportunities.

Calculated risks can enhance your career. Dumb risks can break it. The trick is to figure out your organization's written and unwritten rules about risk. Find out:

- What happens to people who really say what they mean.
- What kind of power base or support you need to take a risk.

Consider these three simple rules for taking risks:

1. Only risk what you can do without.
2. Avoid risking too much for too little.
3. Maximize the odds in your favor.

Most people are afraid to take risks. But keep your fears in perspective. Use the "worst case/probable outcome" technique presented in Chapter 3 to rein in your fears and evaluate the likely (not the unlikely!) consequences of your action.

Whatever you do, don't just stick your head in the sand. Avoiding failure is not the same as seeking success. Neither is conformity. If you never break out of the ranks, you're sure to always be mediocre.

For example, if your boss has decided to tackle a new, high-risk project, and you give it only token effort, don't expect to share in the glory if it succeeds.

**Avoiding failure is not the same
as seeking success**

Help your boss manage change

Planners create. Change-resisters vegetate. When an opportunity to change presents itself, help your boss manage it. Don't run from change. Jump in there and shape it. If you don't plan change, your future will be in someone else's hands!

Help your boss pinpoint your company's need for change by answering these questions:

- What is my organization doing that is no longer serving its purpose? Do I know? Do I have evidence? Am I even asking the question?

- What is my work group doing that is not cost-effective or consistent with our organization's priorities?

- What am I doing personally that may be restricting my growth, limiting my future, dulling my competitive edge?

- Are these changes fundamental or cosmetic? If they are cosmetic, what can we do to get to the basics?

"Because we've always done it that way" is no longer a satisfactory answer to any question. But don't wait to be asked why certain procedures are handled in a certain way. Be curious about the routines around you. Look for ways they can be improved. Consider current procedures an invitation to innovate. And when you find a way, tell your boss!

You can also help your boss in this area by helping prevent the turbulence and chaos that can follow too-rapid or ill-planned change. When you enter a period of change, think of its consequences. What can you do to protect your boss or your department from the side effects of change, so that your business can prosper even as the world is spinning?

Practice candor

To keep your relationship on solid ground, be candid with your boss. If you are to respect one another, you need to be able to "tell it like it is" without worrying about guarding your words, your moods or any other artificial barrier between you.

Once you have established a solid, two-way relationship, keep the channel primed.

- Pass along important news as soon as you get it.
- Advise the boss of delays as soon as you suspect them. No excuses—just give a new commitment date, a date by which the project or responsibility will be complete. Then do the work required to minimize the delay.
- Simplify everything as much as possible.
- Be as brief as you can.
- Eliminate gaps in the information needed.
- Don't color everything with your perspectives, opinions and feelings.

- Be honest about critical problems before your boss hears about them from someone else. Don't cover anything up.
- Leave word where you can be reached when you are away from the office during business hours.

Monitor and evaluate your performance

Finally, to maintain your relationship, you need to continually monitor and evaluate your performance.

This doesn't mean pestering everyone you meet with the question "How'm I doing?" like former New York mayor Ed Koch used to do. But it does mean staying alert to what is happening around you, and how you are contributing to it. Above all, it means negotiating measurable performance expectations, especially during your annual performance review—the subject of the next chapter.

How close is too close?

Your relationship with your boss may be so good that it blossoms into a friendship. Watch out! No matter what, your friendship will always be clouded by the fact that one of you is boss. Candor on the job can be great, but you may come to regret those frank moments over cocktails.

If you and your boss are drifting into a friendship, observe these guidelines:

- Try to find out what has happened in your boss's previous boss-employee friendships. Did your boss conduct open, honorable friendships, or did he use friends to advance his own ends, or betray friends to get rid of competition?

- Watch your words. You are talking to your supervisor, even if the conversation takes place on the golf course. Don't say anything about the company that you would not say to him in the office—or anything that could be used against you later.
- Accept invitations occasionally to join your boss's friends for an event, but don't invite your boss to mix with your friends. Why? Because you can't control their behavior.

Don't flaunt your friendship with the boss to your coworkers. Avoid burdening your boss with your personal problems. What your boss knows about your personal life may influence how comfortable he is with giving you responsibilities on the job.

Ideas to build on

Your relationship with your boss is working when you respect and trust each other and look out for each other's best interests. To keep it working:

- Enhance your skills and keep your competitive edge.
- Learn how to take risks, so you can seek out risks that can advance your career, and avoid risks that can harm it.
- Be your boss's ally in change by looking for ways to improve your organization, and helping manage the process once it is underway.
- Do what you can to nurture a strong relationship—but don't be concerned if it doesn't grow into a friendship.

Chapter 12

Manage Your Performance Review

Ideally, both you and your boss should already have a clear picture of how your performance is perceived *before* your annual performance review is conducted. You should have negotiated performance expectations in advance and agreed upon performance measures. But, to be sure your review is a two-way street, it's essential that you be an active participant in your review.

All too often, a performance review is a one-sided process. Your boss evaluates *you*, while you sit quietly listening to her comments, praises and criticisms and sign off on the written documentation. A fair performance review should allow you, the employee, to have a say as well—to contribute your own self-evaluation and to respond to your boss's comments.

A fair performance review process:

- Is based on previously agreed-upon expectations and objectives.

- Tracks measurable success indicators (quality, quantity, cost, time, etc.).
- Becomes the basis for future development.
- Provides for employee feedback.

An unfair or negative performance review process will have these elements:

- All power is vested in the boss.
- The boss criticizes, and the employee defends.
- The evaluation is based on judgment and opinions.
- It includes few if any measurable criteria.

A positive performance review process is the foundation for charting an individual's progress and determining whether the company's plans hold water. A negative review system leaves most people dejected and depressed. Worse yet, it can restrain innovation and make people afraid to try new things—a sure path to mediocrity.

How to prepare for your performance review

If you are faced with a "top-down" (your boss normally does all the talking) performance review, try asking your boss if you could present her with your self-appraisal after she is finished. Better still, suggest submitting a self-evaluation form before the formal review. This way, you can remind your boss of specific accomplishments she may not have considered, and positively influence the outcome.

That means bringing up your accomplishments in the past year, objectively reviewing your strengths and weaknesses, candidly admitting to things that went wrong and mutually determining your future course.

A performance review should not be a spur-of-the-moment conversation. Both parties need to prepare for it thoughtfully. It is *not* the time to be casual. It is the time to share what you know about yourself and let your boss know how you feel about your accomplishments and shortcomings.

Review your results

Take some time to write down your accomplishments for the past year. What are you particularly proud of? How did your achievements benefit your company? Be sure to quantify your results as much as possible. That is, don't just identify that you exceeded your sales quotas, for example. Indicate how much you exceeded quota and the revenue dollars you brought to the company. Or, instead of indicating that your management efforts streamlined production processes, identify how much money these changes saved your department.

Know your strengths and weaknesses

If you haven't yet developed a good sense of your strengths and weaknesses, this is the perfect time to do so. Go back and do the exercises in Chapter 1. When you're in your review, be candid about your strengths, and honest about your weaknesses. Engaging your boss in a conversation about how you can improve skills will be much more constructive for both of you.

Define your picture of success

Be ready to explain what success means to you, both personally and on the job. How important is money to you?

Leisure time? Family activities? Hobbies? Professional recognition? Job titles? Privileges?

Get feedback from stakeholders and peers

Some companies are beginning to evaluate employees by asking a panel of internal customers and other "stakeholders" to answer questions about their performance.

You can do this yourself by asking a couple of your internal customers for feedback on what you do well and what you need to change. Try not to stack the deck with people who are bound to be on your side. Seek a balance between your fans and those whose praise may not be quite so ardent. You may learn something!

Go through the same exercise with your co-workers. What suggestions do they have for your improvement? In companies with self-directed work teams, peer review is common. It's another reason to treat everyone honorably. You never know who will end up reviewing you!

Gather important materials

Take the time to review sources of information about your performance that can refresh your grasp of your company's basic objectives. Don't overlook documents that establish your department's direction. Consider bringing these with you to the meeting:

- Past performance appraisals.
- Key memos, letters or directives.
- Pertinent company reports.
- Quotas, budgets and forecasts.
- A list of training sessions you have attended.

Develop a personal improvement plan

Before you enter your review session, spend some time reflecting on how you need to improve, and develop a plan for doing so. Use the Competitive Edge Profile in Chapter 11 to pinpoint areas where you need work and to draw up a reasonable plan for getting it done. Be sure to include what *you* need from your boss to help you improve and achieve your goals. Then, when talk turns to the future, you'll be ready.

Determine your worth

How do benefit your company? That's an important question—and its answer can boost your self-esteem before, during and after your performance review. Determine what you really bring to your job and your company. Don't think in terms of what you do; think in terms of the benefits your actions reap. In other words, if you are a copywriter, you don't just write copy. You help your company sell thousands of units of your product every year. If you are the executive assistant to the vice president of sales, then you're the one who helps him stay focused on achieving next year's $12 million sales goal.

Consider what you were really hired to accomplish. Have you done it? Think results, not activities—and when your review begins, *talk* results. Relate your personal performance to objectives the company wants to accomplish.

Think results, not activities

Look ahead

To prepare yourself for discussions about the future, think about the tasks or projects you would like to tackle next year. What would you like to do? What would you just as soon delegate to someone else? Why?

How to manage the review meeting

To get in the right frame of mind before your review starts, remind yourself that your boss probably doesn't enjoy this any more than you do! Most bosses are uncomfortable making judgments about their employees, especially if they are uncertain about their judgments. That's why they will delay conducting the review session as long as they can.

These suggestions will help make your review a positive experience.

1. Sell yourself! You're entitled to tell your boss about what you think you do well. Turn the talk to your talents, and let your light shine. Put in a plug for what you do well!

2. If your boss brings up your mistakes, don't defend them. If they happened, admit it. Explain why they happened and what steps you have taken so that they will not be repeated.

3. Set joint expectations. You and your boss need to set up mutually acceptable goals for your performance. The Personal Performance Contract on pages 168 and 169 is an excellent way to capture and record key results.

4. When your review comes to a close, stand head and shoulders above the crowd by thanking your boss for her time and effort.

5. Write up the results of your review and give a copy to your boss to make sure you agree on its contents and recommendations. Detail the goals you drafted, the measurements you chose, and the time period in which the goals are to be attained. Include any other pertinent details you discussed, such as points needing improvement.

6. Be proactive. Ask your boss for another review in six months to see how you are doing on your goals. She'll probably be surprised and pleased that you want to repeat the process again so soon!

Performance reviews can change opinions—or confirm opinions. Plan for yours carefully so it confirms what has actually happened and sets a course for future improvement.

Let your review confirm what has actually happened and set a course for future improvement.

Negotiate a Personal Performance Contract

Ask your boss to work with you to draw up a Personal Performance Contract—a document that classifies needs, notes the importance of each one, anticipates obstacles, defines performance targets and progress measurements and, most importantly, sets an action plan for *who* will do *what* by *when*.

The first step in the process is to agree on the key results for your job. For example, you and your boss may decide that the three key results you are to achieve in the coming year are to:

- Respond to customer inquiries.
- Spend more time with your most profitable clients.
- Gather and learn from marketplace feedback.

Next, determine how your progress will be measured. Indicators are best expressed in terms of quality, quantity, time and cost. Sample indicators include:

Quantity

- Number of customers/clients served per month, quarter, etc.
- Number of items processed per week, month, etc.
- Number of cases handled.
- Number of customer complaints per year.

Quality

- Error rate/ratio (by department, project, etc.).
- Production hours lost due to injury per quarter, year, etc.
- Percentage of orders without error.
- Percentage of tests repeated.
- Percentage of work redone.

Time

- Number or percentage of deadlines missed.
- Number or percentage of requests answered within five days.
- Number of days to complete.
- Time elapsed (turnaround time).

Cost

- Percentage of variance from budget.
- Dollars as line item in budget.
- Dollars saved over previous quarter.
- Dollar cost per person contacted or order received.

For each key result area, list:

- The need (be as detailed as you can be).
- Why it is important.
- Its relative importance (should it occupy 50 percent of your time, or only 25 percent?).
- Performance targets/results expected.
- How it will be measured—quality, quantity, time or cost.
- Your action plan (who, what, when) for achieving the result.

Finally, draw up an action plan to designate *who* is to do *what* by *when* in order to accomplish your key result. Be sure the plan:

- Details what activity or equipment is needed to achieve the planned objectives.
- Specifies when checkpoints are to be met (dates and deadlines).
- Determines which alternative courses of action should be available.
- Names all responsible people involved.

SAMPLE

PERSONAL PERFORMANCE CONTRACT WORKSHEET

For: **Manufacturing**

Key Result Area	Safety	Security	Supplies	Production Scheduling	Cost Control
Need	Lost time due to accidents up 30% in 1st Qtr.	Eliminate Employee theft.	Stock outages delaying shipments.	Reduce back-order delays to 3 work days.	Reduce departmental expenses by 15% during 2nd quarter.
Why Important	Insurance costs up 60% in past 2 years. Paid time off increasing.	Inventory loss was $55,000 last quarter.	Lost 4 customers last month with total orders of $185,000.	Losing key customers.	Profits must be improved.
How Important %	10%	10%	15%	40%	25%
	100%				
Potential Obstacles	Finding a new insurance carrier. Supervisors are indifferent.	Most material is in unrestricted storage areas.	Unreliable vendors. No inspections in receiving dept.	Cost of new equipment. Employee resistance.	Vendor prices too high & competition limited.

(cont.)

(page 2)

Key Result Area	Safety	Security	Supplies	Production Scheduling	Cost Control
Performance Targets/Results Expected	Reduce frequency rate by 10% this quarter. Reduce severity rate by 12% this quarter.	Reduce inventory loss by 50% in 3 months.	Get new vendors. Assign inspector to receiving dept.	Automate component assembly on line 1 & 2 by 9/1.	Bid costs on all components. Locate minimum of three new suppliers.
Measures Quality/Quantity Time, Cost	# & % of incident reports prepared next day. Manhours lost. Cost to correct unsafe conditions.	# incidents of theft $ amount of missing material.	# days to complete # customers regained. % of shipment rejected. $ value of shipments delayed.	Deadline missed by product. % customers retained. Startup date met?	% improvement upon completion.
Action Plan (Who, What, When)	Leslie B.-prepare weekly report beginning 4/1. Mark D.-recommend corrective action by 5/1 Sam S.-implement by 6/30.	Susan M.-recommend action by 4/1. Jack C.-provide locked storage for priority materials by 4/15.	Nancy G.-get new vendor by 4/20. Tom H.-select and train new inspector by 4/30.	Jane N.-prepare report by 5/1. Max R.-approve plan by 5/12. Joe P.-complete automation project by 6/30.	Jim T-propose bid specs by 4/10. John T-approve by 4/15. Frank O.-implement by 5/20.

This contract is for the period _____ to _____
                                     (mth/day/yr)   (mth/day/yr)

Signed _____

Signed _____
                                     (supervisor)

Ideas to build on

Performance reviews are not a time for surprises. They must be useful for *both* partners. Both should be involved in the process from the beginning to the end.

Once your Personal Performance Contract is in place, use it to monitor your work. Track each month to see whether the steps required to achieve your results are being implemented, by you or by people you supervise.

Make this a time to plan your future together! If you are passive, you will encourage mistakes. If your boss fails to take your views into account, she risks missing your full potential.

Chapter 13

When It's Not Working

This book provides tools with which to turn around a situation that may initially seem unworkable...you and your boss have opposing work styles, your boss seems to ignore you, pick on you, avoid giving you responsibility, hang over your shoulder or set you up to fail. To survive you must be able to turn around a bad situation, and develop a successful working relationship with your boss. In most cases, if you have the knowledge you can achieve great improvement.

However, there are times when a bad relationship with your boss can't be turned around. In this chapter we'll talk about how to recognize those situations and the steps to take to get out of them with minimum damage.

But is it *really* over?

Before you walk out the door, why not take a second look at factors that may be creating an untenable situation? If you can identify them, you can take a stab at correcting them.

Start by analyzing your situation. Is there anything you haven't tried? Has a co-worker succeeded where you have failed? Have you made as many mistakes as the boss? Should you share the guilt for the breakdown?

Check to make sure you really understand what your boss needs. When you do, there may be a chance of supplying it before you find yourself out on the street.

Liking each other is not the problem

Many a disgruntled employee will tell you, "The boss just doesn't like me." But you weren't hired to be liked. You were hired to perform.

It isn't necessary to expect you and your boss to like each other. The point is not to be liked, but to be respected and to accomplish what you are expected to do. "Not being liked" may just be an excuse for not accomplishing what you should.

Focus on becoming allies, not friends.

Before you quit because your boss doesn't like you, ask yourself whether you have truly done everything you can to have him respect you. Have you:

- Been productive in the areas and on the projects that matter most to him?

- Pitched in to help him overcome work-related crises?

- Looked at your own motivations to see whether a past relationship might be influencing this one?

- Observed and tried to emulate the work style of colleagues the boss does like?
- Asked respected co-workers for their interpretation of your situation?

If none of these steps helps, meet with your boss and discuss your concerns. Avoid sounding accusing, but ask what you can do to make the situation better. Tell your boss you're aware that there's a problem. Ask how you are not meeting expectations and what you must do to meet them.

Your boss won't like you just because you're friendly. But he will respect you when he knows that you are prepared to be a team player instead of a buddy. Focus on becoming allies, not friends.

Warning signs: When it's time to go

Yet if the opportunity for damage control is long past, you may be wisest to move on—before that decision is out of your control. If you suspect that your boss has already made the decision to fire you, demote you or move you to a dead-end position in the department or company, it's in your best interest to get out first. Such a termination or a downward move on your resume is always an uncomfortable thing to address during your next job interview. Here are some surefire warning signs that your boss is considering such a severe action.

1. You've had more than one negative performance evaluation.
2. Your boss avoids assigning you projects of any importance—and may be avoiding you altogether.
3. Your boss has starting passing on many of your responsibilities to another individual in the department.

4. You've been left out of important strategy meetings that you used to be invited to.

5. You notice your boss spending more time with others and less time with you.

6. You find your boss giving you information too late to be useful.

7. You are no longer selected to serve on important committees, projects or task forces.

8. In a crisis or emergency, your boss turns to other people, not you.

9. Appraisal sessions lead you to conclude your boss would prefer someone else in your job.

Looking for greener pastures

In the final analysis, you may determine that your job and your career under your current boss is not salvageable. But that doesn't mean you shouldn't put some care and thought into how you make your exit. It's important not to "burn your bridges," to act professionally up to the minute you make your departure. Here are a few recommendations:

- Give your boss adequate notice of your departure—typically, at least two weeks.

- Don't put anything in your resignation letter that could reflect badly on you. Don't blame your boss or criticize the company. It's best to simply refer to your desire to "seek new challenges," and to thank your boss and the company for past opportunities you've enjoyed.

- Do everything you can to make your departure as easy as possible for your boss. Help train your replacement, document procedures for others to follow, make information and files accessible, and provide any other information your boss may need to make the transition a smooth one.

- If your company holds an exit interview with departing employees, keep your comments positive. There's little point in attacking your boss here—rather than help improve the situation for your former co-workers, it will make you appear as a complainer, and may come back to haunt you if you use the company as a reference later on.

Most of us define our expectations of bosses in negative terms. When we leave a job, we say, "I won't ever work for anyone like that again." We have a clear sense of what we won't put up with, but are not as clear on what to look for and how we must change.

When you move on to new opportunities, spend some time finding out about the various bosses you may end up working for. In terms of your overall career, a good boss can be just as valuable as challenging work, great pay or flexible hours. To pick a winner, look for a boss with these characteristics:

- Identifies employee strengths and builds on them.
- Criticizes privately, and praises publicly.
- Values change.
- Does not punish initiative and risk-taking.
- Encourages constructive criticism.
- Honors those who persist.
- Negotiates plans of action to meet objectives.
- Establishes accountabilities for every position and every employee—*who* will do *what* by *when*.

- Does not accept results below agreed-upon standards.
- Rewards performance, not mediocrity.

Ideas to build on

If all else fails, leave. Move on. Don't waste your life trying to reform a tyrant who wouldn't change if hit with a bolt of lightning. Even in these tumultuous times, there is another job for you. Don't be afraid to find it. When you have a better boss, you can try again.

Section V

Do You Know These Bosses?

If you're working for a good boss, you already know it. Author Leo Tolstoy once wrote that "Happy families are all alike; every unhappy family is unhappy in its own way." While not all good bosses are the same kind of people, their effect on their employees can be summed up in a few key phrases:

- They help you get where you want to go.
- They take time to listen.
- They delegate, make full use of their staff's resources.
- They take chances.
- They make coming to work fun.
- They add a sense of purpose and excitement to even the most mundane assignments.
- They build loyal teams.
- They're strong leaders and good role models.

But even good bosses have some bad habits or behaviors. It's not unusual for inspiring, charismatic bosses to have a king-size ego, or for technical geniuses to be aloof toward their staff. It all comes with the territory. But too generous a helping of bad habits and behaviors adds up to a bad boss.

Let's dig a little deeper to find out more about your boss:

- Does your boss consistently avoid promoting people from your department into positions of higher authority?
- Have any charges of sexual harassment ever been brought against your boss?
- Is there a high turnover of personnel in your department?

- Does your boss talk disparagingly about people behind their backs?
- Does your boss use anger to intimidate people?
- Is your boss competitive in conversation, having to always "one-up" others?
- Does your boss steal credit from staff for projects they complete?
- Do talented employees seem to be a threat to your boss?

If you answered "yes" to more than a couple of these, it's likely you're stuck with a bad boss.

How bad your boss is can be measured by how much he squelches your career, either by blocking your career moves, taking credit for your achievements or undermining your credibility. If you've networked effectively within your company and have friends in high places, you might be able to tolerate your bad boss until you can transfer to a good one. If, however, your boss is involved in unethical behavior or sexual harassment, or is "bending" the law, you really can't afford to continue working for him.

Read the next chapter to determine just what kind of boss you have, and to discover and adopt effective strategies for managing him. Bad bosses— well, you must find ways to manage that relationship until you can cut your losses and move on. In addition, these lessons will help you in the future if you become "the boss."

Chapter 14

A Gallery
of Bosses

The tough boss

We can be thankful that, as a trend, the tough, dictatorial management style is becoming obsolete. But it still typifies a lot of bosses who believe it's okay to brutalize their employees in an effort to force peak performance out of them.

If you've got a tough, angry boss, time is on your side. The shrinking labor pool of the '90s has forced managers to put more emphasis on valuing employees rather than browbeating them. Yet, the planned obsolescence of the tough, angry boss doesn't make your job any easier—especially when he overworks, underpays and publicly berates employees.

Tough bosses are often valued by those above them, while those below them suffer. They manage to get the job done and to meet bottom-line requirements. Your tough boss may have support, even full approval, from upper management. Therefore, he's in an ideal position to do some real damage to his employees by discrediting them. Just what can he do to you?

Undermine your credibility. As far as the company is concerned, your main "window on the world" is through your boss. If your boss doesn't like you or is secretly afraid of you, he can tarnish your record, deny your contribution and do his utmost to make sure no other boss in the company will welcome you into his or her department.

Block your career through an accusatory review. The performance review is frequently the big showdown, where—after a year of hard work—you can walk away with more money and a promotion...or absolutely zero. A tough, angry boss may try to slow your career growth by submitting you to an accusatory review.

Such bosses do not like to reward employees—even hardworking ones. They derive power from throwing others off-balance and keeping them guessing. Rather than recognizing your achievements and contributions, your tough boss will berate you with your failures and shortcomings. Money is another big control issue with this type of boss, so he'll probably give you as little as possible.

What can you do?

Such bosses are essentially bullies who enjoy intimidating employees. Their arrogance, however, does create a few blind spots. Your boss probably overestimates his control, not only over his employees but with lateral bosses as well.

You need the chance to prove your worth to someone other than this tyrant. Look around. Surely not every boss in your company believes your boss is such a great guy. Some are probably as put off by his arrogance, unfairness and intimidation as you are.

- See if there is a neutral party you can talk to: a company ombudsman, an employee assistance program.
- Make sure your job performance is good; keep records of your accomplishments, attendance and productivity.
- When the opportunity arises, seek a transfer within the company—to a better boss.
- Finally, stand up to your boss when he is abusive or tries to intimidate you. If he makes accusations, insist that he back up his comments with facts. If he tries to intimidate you through implied or direct threats regarding your job security, tell him your work record will speak for itself and you'll be happy to discuss the matter before a review board or a mediating organization.

You can short-circuit the effects of the accusatory review by going into the meeting prepared with documentation of your achievements. Have at least one witness present. Bullies don't like to go public unless they are sure of their support. If your boss is allowed to prevail and you know he's being unfair, don't try to confront him. Such a boss thrives on personal conflict and verbal abuse. You'll only come out bruised and battered. Several courses of action are open to you. One is to go to your boss's boss. Another is to file a grievance.

When you go over your boss's head you've declared war, so be prepared for a vindictive response. Various schools of thought exist about when it's appropriate to go over your boss's head. They are:

1. Never. It violates the chain of command. Other bosses view it as insubordination.
2. Sometimes. But only go to lateral bosses, never to his boss.
3. Situational. When you have no alternative, go to his boss.

If you're going to complain to a higher authority, make sure you do it properly. Make an appointment beforehand, have proper documentation. If possible, have tape recordings or notes in your boss's handwriting to refute any possible charges that you've manufactured the evidence. Let your boss know the action you are taking.

The purpose of going to your boss's boss or to a boss in another department is to hold your boss accountable, since he feels no need for accountability to employees.

If your boss's boss does not resolve the situation to your satisfaction, you're entitled to file a grievance. You can also file grievance procedures outside the company, which are handled through laws regarding equal opportunity and unfair labor practices. Both are covered in Chapter 15, "Strategies to Stop Bad Bosses."

The charismatic boss

People love a winner. They like voting for winning presidents, betting on winning horses, playing on winning teams. That's because winning is infectious. People like being around highly charismatic leaders because some of their positive energy rubs off.

A charismatic leader can be a terrific team builder, obliterating differences and integrating opposing forces into a powerful group. A charismatic leader works most effectively with her team when she is accessible to team members. Without accessibility, motivation can quickly fade.

Perform well and your charismatic boss can do a lot for you. Perhaps she sees possibilities in you that far exceed her own accomplishments. She can tell you what pitfalls to avoid, what shortcuts will only derail your career. A charismatic boss:

- Lets her self-confidence inspire self-confidence in you.
- Makes a dull job fun.
- Communicates a sense of mission.
- Makes you proud to be on her team.
- Values and understands your contributions and can increase your visibility within the company *and* the community.

The downside is that they usually trust their charismatic influence too much. They try to "talk their way out" of situations when expertise is required.

What can you do?

Sooner or later, charismatic leaders, just like less dramatic managers, have to become team players, not just team owners. To be effective, they must also be able to demonstrate they can plan a crusade as well as lead one.

It's not unusual for highly charismatic people to be ineffective at detail work, organizing and intensive planning.

Find out where your boss's weaknesses are, then offer badly needed support.

With a charismatic boss, you can:

- Take charge. Be self-motivating. She's not interested in supervising daily routines.

- Master the details of running the office.

- Make your boss look good. Give her support where she needs it and keep her public image intact.

- Give her feedback. She needs to know how staff members feel.

- Share your expertise with your boss. She needs to learn new information constantly.

The competitive boss

Bosses compete with employees in all sorts of ways, openly and behind the scenes. Men traditionally compete with each other, both as bosses of younger male employees, and with their executive peers. Male employees are often plunged into fierce competition by top-performing female co-workers and bosses. If you're a woman with a female boss, a certain amount of friction already exists. In a recent study, 47 percent of the women polled said they would prefer to work for a man and 44 percent of the men polled said their boss's gender made no difference.

Many women report that they compete against women more fiercely and for far less rewards than men compete against men. If you're female and you have a competitive female boss, you might want to ask yourself these questions:

- What is it that we compete most strongly for? Money, attention, expertise?
- What does my boss have to gain from making her employees look bad?
- How do other bosses see me? Is my boss hurting my career, or am I expected to deal with her and move on?

Both men and women bosses can be competitive. And both can be equally hard to deal with. The best approach to dealing with a competitive boss is to find ways to promote teamwork with your boss and create a relationship built on trust rather than competition.

What can a competitive boss do to you? Take credit for your achievements, for one thing. Unless your achievements are documented and on file, your boss may try stealing your ideas and then stealing your credit and promotion. Competitive, unscrupulous bosses look for talented, inexperienced employees who will mistake their interest in them for true appreciation.

What can you do?

You will probably have to let the incident pass the first time it happens. But if it looks like your boss is developing a pattern of taking credit for your achievements, you can:

- Document to others your participation in projects, particularly to other bosses or your boss's boss, if possible. Do this through reports and memos written by you; active participation in meetings; working late and coming in early to work on a project and making sure other bosses see you and know what you're working on; suggesting an article be written in the employee newsletter (if appropriate) on your project; and saving any memos or correspondence that may support and document your role.

- Push for visibility and recognition elsewhere. Realize that you may never get your boss to acknowledge your participation.
- Meet with your boss privately when he blatantly refuses to recognize your involvement (not listing your name as the author or participant in a project). Call the omission to his attention. Ask for the error to be corrected.

The delegating boss

As companies grow, bosses get busier. Good bosses quickly learn the value of delegating responsibility to subordinates—before their departments feel the effects of their many commitments. Some bosses have to be pressured into delegating, others seize upon the opportunity.

A boss who delegates well delegates fairly—giving all team members a shot at assignments that can increase their share in the credit. Delegation also fosters a team's confidence in its leader to prioritize: knowing which projects are crucial, which can be handed around, which call for immediate action. Finally, the delegating boss trusts those who work for her, causing staff to produce more, offer honest feedback and develop into highly skilled employees.

Your delegating boss can:

- Show you she thinks you're good enough to be trusted with important responsibility.
- Give you a chance to prove yourself on a new project.
- Take full advantage of your talents.
- Groom you for promotion by increasing your visibility to upper-level management.

Beware, however, of the boss who:

- Delegates without giving you information or authority.
- Dumps only insignificant tasks on you.
- Tells you an assignment is really important when it is not.
- Traps you into thinking that you will be rewarded for completing a delegated job and then forgets it.

What can you do?

Your delegating boss has shown her confidence in you by giving you important projects. Her trust is both stimulating and stress-producing. It's a test you don't want to fail, yet perhaps you lack information or expertise to perform with confidence.

Keep in close touch. Your boss has delegated to you, not only because she's busy but because she knows you're ready. Don't hesitate to:

- Ask plenty of questions, get information.
- Give her feedback on your approach.
- Don't complain about not having enough time for your "regular job."

- Show her you're trustworthy by constantly doing what you say you will do.
- Meet deadlines.
- Accept criticism.

The dependent boss

Some bosses will use the intimacy that results from daily working relationships to establish an emotional dependency in which the employee becomes a substitute authority figure of the parental variety.

At first, you may welcome what appears to be your boss's trust and confidence, and eagerly respond with advice or interested observations. Eventually, however, the boss's dependency interferes with the work that needs to be done and you finally see that you are placed in a compromising relationship. Not only is it unprofessional, but emotionally draining as well. To back off may seem like career suicide, but to encourage such an exchange is equally harmful.

What can you do?

Try to determine if your boss is going through a particularly difficult phase either in his career or at home. You might want to bear with him until the pressure eases off. If his behavior seems to be neurotic, however, don't think twice about ending your involvement. Chances are, if you create some distance, he will find another sympathetic ear.

Set limits on your time and the kind of topics you're willing to discuss. If you need to discuss business with your boss and he wanders off the subject, listen politely, then firmly bring him back to the subject. You can try nonverbal communication like looking at your watch or simply say, *"Did we reach a decision about how we're handling the sales reports?"*

The disorganized boss

The disorganized boss may look to you to organize her time. Her office is a disaster area. She may keep few or sloppy records, have no sense of priorities and may not even be sure what her calendar for the day looks like—but she expects you to help clean up the messes and keep the work going out.

Her slipshod approach to communicating may mean you miss out on important information or opportunities. (Others may cut her out of the loop because of her disorganization.) You risk burnout if all your attention is devoted to putting out fires instead of the happier, more rewarding tasks of planning strategy and seeing results.

On the other hand, you may find yourself in a position of real power—but you will need to make sure that your efforts are recognized.

What can you do?

- Know the goals and priorities of your organization and use them to help keep the disorganized boss on track.
- Offer suggestions in a tone that indicates you really want to be helpful. Use soft phrases like "I

wonder what would happen if we tried doing..." to suggest new approaches or take over neglected responsibilities.

- Make it easy for your boss to delegate to you duties that slow her down.

- If you think you are missing out on important information, you may need to go to others outside your department.

- Create and maintain a mental picture of an organized office, and do all you can to achieve it.

The drug or alcohol abuser

Twenty years ago, two martinis at lunch were part of a powerful boss's minimum daily requirement. Times have changed and so has the public's awareness of the damage caused by drugs and alcohol. Yet, some upper-level managers have found themselves unwittingly trapped in a cycle of substance dependency that began as an effort to numb the stress they encountered in their jobs.

Sometimes it's difficult to tell if drugs or alcohol use is becoming a problem for your boss—drug use, especially, because an individual is most likely going to hide evidence of such use, whereas you might observe if a boss drinks too much at lunch. Here are some warning signs that drug or alcohol abuse may be a problem:

- Your boss regularly comes to work late.

- He may arrive at work looking ill, with red eyes or runny nose.

- He takes long lunches.
- You or other co-workers observe that he drinks too much at lunch or at work-related functions.
- He frequently falls asleep at his desk.
- He exhibits drastic shifts in moods, even in a single morning.
- He exhibits shoddy work performance, little follow-through.
- He is abusive toward employees.
- He presents extremes in mood, which may include depression, manic energy, apathy, inability to concentrate.
- Your boss reveals he has family problems or financial problems.

What can you do?

- Many companies now have special programs for drug or alcohol dependent employees. Find out if your company has such a program.
- Find out who is the best, most receptive person with whom you can discuss this problem. It may be a human resource manager or an employee assistance specialist. Be careful. Be sure of your facts.
- Have your facts clearly documented. Present the information with compassion for your boss and from the standpoint that you're doing what's best for him and the company.
- Finally, request confidentiality. If your supporting evidence is convincing, there's no reason for you to become involved any further.

Warning: This is a very volatile situation. Proceed with caution. Don't act on rumors. If facts reveal a problem, express your concern to your boss first before exposing the problem to anyone else.

The incompetent boss

An incompetent boss likes to delay any kind of decisions as long as possible. She hates to demonstrate strong leadership and thinks only in terms of avoidance rather than creative solutions. Innovation is the bane of her existence—so is conflict. She avoids hiring and firing employees, performance reviews, soliciting employee feedback and meeting project deadlines.

To mask her incompetence, this kind of boss will form committees, set up fact-finding studies and hire outside consultants. But the real problems never get resolved because the incompetent boss neither listens nor learns.

Often, incompetent bosses have been promoted from areas within the company where they had some real technical expertise. They might have been more comfortable working as "independent contributors" than as team leaders; thus they tend to panic when management skills are required.

If you work for a boss who's incompetent, chances are she's still got her job because her boss knows she's no threat and wants your boss exactly where she is. Or your boss may have "connections" at the higher levels of management. You'll recognize incompetent bosses by their:

- Avoidance of conflict at any cost.
- Tendency to interrupt others, drone on, not listen, avoid eye contact.

- Fear of more capable employees who might take their jobs or expose their inadequacies.
- Inability to grasp the essentials required for acceptable job performance.

What can you do?

If you think you're working for an incompetent boss, compare notes with co-workers. How do they react to this supervision? Look for facts, not opinions or gossip. Find out, if you can, what your boss's track record is with your company and with former companies. Does she change jobs a lot? Complain of having been mistreated and unfairly dealt with? If so, it's likely that other companies realized her incompetence and took action.

Try to determine how soon, if at all, your incompetent boss will be led to the company's chopping block. Ask yourself:

1. Will upper management eventually wake up and do something about my boss?
2. Is it possible for me to make my boss's inadequacies known?
3. What is my track record with this company? Would my criticism be believed?
4. Can I risk being labeled a complainer by upper management?
5. Can I afford having this person as my manager?

Executives often look bad if they promote or protect incompetent bosses. However, it might not be to your advantage to complain about your incompetent boss. Therefore, you may have to work with her, support her, organize her and do her job.

If you work for an incompetent boss, try to keep her out of situations in which she becomes a laughing stock. You may be tempted to expose her—but it's better to do what you can to prevent an embarrassing error.

You can make the most of a bad situation by asking for more responsibility and turning the incompetent boss into an ally by being truly helpful.

By carefully documenting your work for your incompetent boss you may be able to get yourself promoted and transferred into another department.

The indifferent boss

Indifferent bosses cast a cloud of listlessness that is difficult for even the most eager subordinates to overcome. Perhaps their indifference stems from a woefully botched job of corporate miscasting. Rather than heading up a market research department, for instance, your boss may have preferred a position with higher visibility—say as head of sales. In any case, his apathy shows; and unless you're careful, you could end up being just like your boss—indifferent.

Ask yourself the following questions to determine the extent of your boss's indifference:

1. Does your boss use the bureaucracy as an excuse for not doing anything: ("I'd really like to help you out, but the company policy manual says...").

2. Is your boss worn out from too many years on the fast track?

3. Is he experiencing too many conflicting priorities: career, family, health and money?

4. Is he cynical?
5. Does he discourage any attempts at team-building?
6. Does he discourage feedback?

Nothing is more deflating than being stuck with an indifferent boss. He usually holds onto his position through seniority or some quirk of expertise.

What can you do?

If your boss is burned out from too much job-related travel, family pressures or spending nearly every weekend at the office, encourage him to open up and look at some options. Perhaps he could consider scheduling a morale-building weekend retreat for the whole department, a motivational seminar, or weekly staff meetings to encourage feedback.

Remember, your boss's lack of caring permeates the entire department. Perhaps his shell of indifference is his way of protecting his job from ambitious staff people. Ask yourself:

1. Is he really indifferent, depressed and uncaring or is this some kind of defense mechanism?
2. Does his behavior continue at home or in the community, or does it change when he leaves the office?
3. How does working for him affect my pride in my work?
4. Do other bosses in the company value his work?
5. Is my boss merely a poor leader?
6. Can I find something about my boss's performance that is outstanding, and compliment him on that?
7. Is he threatened by employees who are achievers?
8. Does my boss suffer from low self-esteem?

Many employees find that the greatest joy comes not just from performing their jobs well, but from the high morale that results from teamwork. When your boss denies you these benefits, it's difficult to keep up the quality of your work. In this case, you must evaluate how much longer you can afford to work for such a boss without your own attitude slipping. If he is capable of change—that is, if his attitude is the result of a specific incident and not habitual—do you want to get involved in helping him recover? Assess who else is aware of the situation and who in the company can provide guidance for you.

The intimidating boss

An intimidating boss may actually be hiding behind a facade designed to scare off staff who might offer unwanted suggestions. Behind those intimidation tactics lurks someone whose low self-esteem will not accept criticism of any kind, no matter how kindly it is offered. Bosses who feel powerless often try to intimidate their employees in an attempt to exhibit their control.

Intimidators try to keep you "in your place" by increasing your sense of insecurity. They will constantly remind you that they outrank you and that you are dependent upon them.

Typically, they'll not value your suggestions and try to make you feel inadequate. They will remind you of your mistakes but never recognize your achievements.

What can you do?

- No matter how angry you feel, try to remain in control of your reactions. Your overly intimidating boss isn't simply in search of a way to complete a task; she also wants a reaction. If you can give her the work she wants minus the reaction, she may take her upsetting tactics elsewhere.

- Try to become aware of where your boss's self-esteem is lacking. Then look at ways in which you can bolster it without being obviously manipulative.

- Check to see who else she intimidates and determine if the reasons seem to be the same.

- If this treatment becomes intolerable, carefully prepare for a meeting in which you give examples of her intimidating style and its effect on you.

The moody boss

A boss who goes through several mood changes each hour isn't necessarily making unreasonable emotional demands on you. He's simply at the mercy of his own emotions and can't help displaying them at inappropriate times. If his spirits plummet from congeniality to black despair and back up again, keep in mind that his reactions aren't based on anything you've done.

What can you do?

First, don't take his reactions personally. Secondly, give him some feedback. Based on how open your relationship with your boss is, let him know how his moods affect clients, co-workers and upper management. It might be a behavior he's not aware of and can change.

Timing and anticipation are the keys to working with your moody boss. Try to anticipate when he's most open, and when he's not. When you have to bring him bad news, time your message carefully. You may feel like you're constantly walking on eggshells with this boss, but the payoff is worth it.

Keep track of his moods for a few weeks. You may discover he's always grumpy and irritable in the morning, so avoid morning meetings whenever you can. Or, you may find out that his mood changes quickly when you agree to do something he hates to do, so take as much delegated work as you can. You may discover you are ready for promotion much sooner than you think by using his moodiness to your advantage.

The motivating boss

A motivating boss is a mentor in the highest sense of the word. It's no surprise that bosses who motivate others are good at communicating their interest in their staff. Employees want bosses who care, who take a sincere interest in them, their families, their lives.

To truly motivate you, a good boss must also help you develop your talent, use your creativity and push you where you want to go. To do this, a motivating boss can either offer to become your mentor or help you network.

Mentoring, or providing "help from above," is a powerful motivator to succeed. It's one way good bosses can show they care about promising employees by lending a helping hand. Mentoring can range from giving detailed guidance and advice to general encouragement. It's a wide-ranging show of support given from a person in a powerful position to an employee over a period of time.

Mentors can move you upward in the corporate organization by:

- Acting as your sponsor.
- Praising you to other bosses.
- Including you in special projects that give you visibility and help you see how the business world works.

A mentor can show you the ropes, cut through corporate red tape and introduce you to sources it would ordinarily take you years to find and cultivate. Mentoring is also a way for a boss to groom a replacement.

A good boss or mentor will also help you build your network of valuable career contacts—which may lead to other opportunities outside of your immediate department or company. Your boss may promote you to other potential employers by selling your abilities. Your boss will be using tools like:

- Your proven track record.
- Evidence of untapped abilities that would be better used in another department or company.
- Knowledge of your overall goals and career plans.

What can you do?

The best way to manage a boss who is a good motivator is to succeed. Live the lessons she's teaching you and show her you're an eager and willing student. Don't disappoint her through unprofessional behavior or an attitude that you've got it made now that she is helping you.

Motivators thrive on enthusiasm, encouragement and feedback. You, in turn, can motivate your boss by:

- Performing well.
- Showing a respectful interest in your boss and her work.
- Learning all you can from her.
- Teaching your boss and sharing the value of your expertise.
- Sharing with her your innovative thinking, your creative solutions.

Use your boss as a role model, a mentor, even as a competitor if that keeps you motivated. The more you show you want to learn, the more she'll teach you.

If you find your opportunities to tap into your boss are limited—perhaps your department is so large, she's not able to spend as much time coaching and guiding you as you'd like—seek a mentor outside the department. Mentors are sometimes bosses in other departments or "experts" in your field.

Sometimes, companies have instituted a formalized structure where aspiring employees can go for executive help.

The "savior"

The door opens, and in walks the new boss. Her first comments indicate she has come to save you and your department from certain disaster. She is obviously very impressed by her own credentials and experience. She criticizes everything about her new environment, constantly referring to how things were done at her former company, till finally, most of her new staff wonders why she even left.

What can you do?

It's important to realize that much of your new boss's behavior may be attributed to nervousness and insecurity on her part. No matter how talented an individual may be, it's always difficult and a little threatening to take on authority in a new environment. Her bravado may just be her way of reassuring herself. You can help her get over this period of uncertainty more quickly—as well as establishing a positive working relationship with your boss by following these steps:

- Receive your boss's suggestions in a positive manner, and don't misinterpret them as criticism.

- Spend some time—at lunch, perhaps—getting her to talk about herself and her past experiences, even personal aspects about herself.

- Evaluate her daily routine. What does she like to do first? Last?

- Find out what tasks she avoids, then base your actions on doing those things for her.

- Volunteer to help her get acquainted.

- Don't complain about other employees—even the bad ones. Let her find out for herself. Otherwise you may be branded as a "blamer" rather than a "doer."

- Don't underrate her. Behave as if you expect her to succeed.

- Don't be suspicious that she will want to replace you with someone she knows better. A suspicious attitude is easy to detect and hard to dispel.

- Find out how she likes to receive good news and bad news and act accordingly.

- Focus on performance, not politics. Believe that in the long run, performance will prevail.
- Determine, as soon as possible, how you can become valuable to your new boss. Do the things that increase your value.

The off-site boss

Thanks to the wonders of telecommunication, many people work in one place while reporting to a boss in another. This sort of long-distance relationship presents challenges you will have to work to overcome. Think about a long-distance romance or friendship, and how much energy it takes to maintain! Your long-distance relationship with your boss will consume just as much energy—or maybe more.

Some problematic situations can arise when you report to a boss who's located someplace else. They include:

- Uncertainty about your priorities.
- Gaps in information.
- Not getting recognition for your accomplishments.
- Not being fairly represented to those above your boss.

What can you do?

To manage your off-site boss:

- Keep him informed. Don't surprise him with bad news.
- Clarify his expectations, then concentrate on the highest priorities.

- Determine the boundaries of your job. For example, is there anyone your boss does *not* want you to contact?
- Negotiate measurable goals and report on your progress regularly (at least weekly).
- Separate major and minor aspects of your work. Delegate as many of the minor ones as you can.
- Gradually wean yourself away from having to report on details.
- Educate your remote boss on why he should trust you. For example, solve problems before he even learns about them.
- Monitor your own progress on the most critical aspects of your job *before* your boss does.
- Take advantage of technology to communicate, including E-mail, fax machines and cellular and car phones.
- Do your job so well that your remote boss needs to spend less time with you than with any of the others who report to him.

The parental boss

Some bosses are most comfortable reliving patterns they learned as children. It seems logical to them, now that they're adults with responsibility for employees, that they assume the role of a parent.

There's the boss who views his staff as a "family" and thinks of himself as the stern, but loving father. Or the female who "mothers" her employees, encouraging them to confide in her. These parental bosses may be well-intentioned, but they've overlooked the glaring fact that the office is not the home. Their behavior is detrimental to all concerned.

It could be that your boss is trying to hang onto power by building a sense of loyalty through guilt. A boss often adopts this kind of behavior to mask a lack of expertise or competence. Be careful how you respond. Choose your remarks carefully. When confronted, a parental boss can drop the parental act and turn mean and nasty in a heartbeat.

Paternalistic bosses who are comfortable assigning women stereotypical roles may view female employees not only as daughters, but wives and mothers as well. Female subordinates may find that paternalistic bosses refuse to take them seriously, preferring instead to patronize them. Male employees may have trouble deflecting numerous queries and advice about their private life by maternalistic bosses.

Through the power of association, other bosses and co-workers in your company may think that you're just as unprofessional and ineffectual as your boss.

Finally, if you excel while working for dad or mom, they may be unwilling to promote you, give you a raise or reward you properly. Your department is just "one big happy family" as far are they're concerned and you've found your place.

What can you do?

Your best strategy is to keep up a professional image in every contact you have with your boss. Be sure to follow some basic guidelines. Otherwise, you'll get derailed:

1. Plan what you intend to say. Be specific and factual, rather than emotional. You don't want to act like a "child."

2. Stay on the subject; reiterate your goals when the conversation goes off course.

3. Don't make jokes, small talk, share personal confidences or spend a lot of time listening to your boss's anecdotes.

4. If your boss starts waffling, provide closure and structure. "A week from Thursday, then, I'm to have the improved sales figures for all my accounts to you for review?"

5. Do everything you can to establish your ability and competence as undeniable—even by a boss who is tempted to treat you as dependent on others.

The powerholic

The only issue these "powerholic" bosses care about is if they're in the driver's seat. Working for them can be a tough assignment. You've got to walk a fine line between being competent enough to make them look good yet not challenging them with your independence or ability.

The key word for powerholics is control. They've got to control everyone and everything around them, no matter how insignificant their place on the corporate pyramid.

Here are some characteristics of powerholics:

- They rarely provide staff with a chance to advance.
- They don't delegate well, claiming their people do such a poor job, "I just have to do it over again myself."
- They're single-minded and ego driven, sacrificing the good of the company for the growth of their own empires.

- They're not receptive to innovation, particularly when their ways of doing things are challenged.
- They're often overbearing, demanding, contemptuous and bullying.

What can you do?

Before devising strategies to use when working with a powerholic, answer these questions.

1. How much power does he really have? Does it reside completely in the position or does he possess some personal power as well?
2. How vital is my department within the corporation? What essential services does it perform?
3. What kind of power does my boss have with his immediate boss? A lot? Or none?
4. Can I make a successful lateral move to another department without damaging my career?

In other words, determine if your boss's power is real or imagined. Companies often give these individuals departments to control that have no real effect on bottom-line profits. If your boss is merely a paper tiger: Try to find out if there's a boss elsewhere in your company with some real power and influence. Then make it clear you'd like to transfer to that department and be given more responsibility.

If your boss really does have power, find out if he's willing to give you a hand up by becoming a mentor. This approach may appeal sufficiently to his ego that he will help you.

Whatever the outcome, look for ways you can learn from the experience—whether it is job skills you're learning or improved interpersonal and management skills.

The sexual harasser

It's not unusual for conflicts to arise when men work for women, or women work for men, in the modern world of business. Although these conflicts may be job-related, they sometimes stem from underlying sexual tension and issues of power. Women bosses can sexually harass male employees, but the occurrences of such behavior are rare compared to the reverse.

Sometimes harassment is not intended, but rather more appropriate for conversation in a locker room. Offensive jokes, language about women, pinups, hugging or comments about a woman's appearance may not be meant to offend, but should be addressed anyway. If you're wondering if your boss's growing attentiveness is out of bounds, ask yourself:

- Does he compliment me or stare unnecessarily at me?
- Does he "accidentally" touch parts of my body?
- Does he stop such behavior when I ask him to?
- Does he pester me by calling me at home?
- Does he threaten me when I reject such inappropriate behavior?
- Does he treat all women as if they were part of his "office harem?"
- Is turnover high among females in his department?
- Does he ask me to stay late and work with him when the project isn't crucial?
- Have charges of sexual harassment ever been brought against him?

Sexual harassment doesn't have to culminate in demands for sex. It also includes any kind of innuendo, teasing, attention to one's dress, excessive touching or pestering that the employee finds unwelcome and inappropriate.

Don't wait to take action. Put a stop to offensive comments by saying "Your remarks/actions are offensive and I want them to stop." Usually, most "innocent" offenders will take the hint and change their behavior.

If your boss is truly making advances toward you, be prepared for lack of cooperation or denial when you ask him to stop. He may consider it all part of the game, that women say "no" when they really mean "yes." And if you go above his head, to his boss or register a formal complaint, be prepared for possible repercussions.

What can you do?

Some companies don't like employees who rock the boat—that includes standing up to a boss who sexually harasses female employees. But even if you end up leaving the company to escape this situation, you'll know that by taking formal action against him—unlike others who silently and swiftly disappeared before—your complaint constitutes the beginning of a record against which your boss's subsequent behavior can be measured.

If your boss has refused to stop his harassment, threatened you either physically or by using your job security as blackmail, you should make your fears known to those who can restrain him. Document and, if possible, tape record his outbursts, threats or innuendoes, then take your case to the big bosses. (For more information, see Chapter 15, "Strategies to Stop Bad Bosses.")

The team-builder boss

Probably the best qualification your boss can have for being truly outstanding is her ability to build a strong, loyal team. If your boss is a good team-builder, she:

- Perceives and fully uses the strengths of each team member.
- Inspires loyalty on behalf of team members by her own accountability.
- Encourages cooperation among team members by emphasizing fair play.
- Can qualify as a hero. (Every team needs one!)

Good team-builders, like good coaches, want players with different abilities to play specific positions. They know the inherent value in diversity—the more diverse a culture, the greater its strength. Therefore, they don't expect all team members to be alike or play alike. A good manager will take the time to listen to her staff members, get to know each one and learn what motivates each one individually and as a part of a team.

By working for a good team-builder, you'll learn how to play as part of a team to accomplish a common goal. By becoming part of the process, you become invested in the outcome. The team's goals become your goals.

When introducing a new project, a good team-builder helps you:

- Understand the importance of the project.
- Appreciate how your involvement is critical and how you will benefit from the project's success.
- Find your own work rhythm.

Most important, you can learn how individual contributions can be incorporated and transformed into an all-consuming group effort. A good coach can get her team to play together by building trust. With trust, groups can gather and process data more quickly, respond to change with greater flexibility.

As a team member, you may also experience more open conflict with team members and with your boss. Yet conflict based on trust can be healthy and constructive. If your boss has built a strong team, it can lead not only to greater creativity and awareness, but to the winning result everyone wants.

What can you do?

As much as your boss may emphasize the equal status of all team members (including herself), each team also needs a leader—someone everyone can respect and respond to. To be an effective coach, your boss needs feedback. The more she has fostered an atmosphere of trust, the more honest feedback you can give her.

1. Let her know your feelings and opinions, even when they conflict with hers.
2. Let her know if she's dictating her wishes to the team rather than listening.
3. Let her know if she's represented your team fairly to upper-level management.
4. Don't take her criticisms personally.
5. Communicate your appreciation when she rewards the team for achieving a mutually defined goal.

Chapter 15

Formal Strategies to Stop Bad Bosses

Confronting a boss is never easy. Confronting a *bad* boss is a lot harder because you have a pretty good idea, before you even start that things will not go well. Most executives won't even listen to your complaints about your bad boss unless you have documented them and confronted the boss first.

Basically, you have two choices—leave the company or take official steps to change your boss or have him removed. This chapter covers the *formal* processes involved in improving a bad-boss situation. Keep in mind however, that there are no guarantees.

Filing a grievance

The grievance procedure varies from company to company. It can be handled informally by the company president holding a meeting with the relevant parties, or formally.

Legally, you're required to file a grievance with your company's human resources director within five working days of the last meeting with your boss's boss. These are the steps:

1. First go to your boss.

2. If you don't get satisfaction, document this meeting and go to your boss's boss—notifying your boss you're doing so.

3. Then, if you don't get satisfaction, you file a legal grievance with the human resources department—after notifying your boss and boss's boss you're doing so.

Consult your human resources department about the categories and process for filing a legal grievance.

Within five working days of receiving the grievance, the human resources director should set up a meeting with you, your boss and your boss's boss in an attempt to reach an agreement.

It sounds like it should work, but it often doesn't. Depending on the amount of power they wield, bad bosses can escape unscathed, while the employees suffer the consequences of going back to work for the boss they've complained about.

Going public

When an employee fails to stop a boss's serious wrongdoing (harassment, racial, gender or sex discrimination, embezzlement, fraud, security violations) by working within the company structure, he or she may choose to go public.

Never go public without hard evidence that supports your complaint. The most common strategies are:

1. **Whistle-blowing.** This means turning your boss in to the media, government agencies or law enforcement officials. Employees who go to this length must be prepared to pay the price of a long, hard public fight. In many cases, by the time the employee takes this drastic step, he or she is no longer employed by the offending company. Sometimes the employee is able to return to his or her job—but most often, too much damage is done to make it comfortable to return to an environment where other employees may perceive the employee as disloyal, dangerous or even demented.

   When whistle-blowers are still employed by their companies, federal laws now make it illegal for employers to retaliate.

2. **Legal Action.** For those disenfranchised employees who thirst not only for vindication but for justice, taking legal action against former employers is now possible thanks to the anti-discrimination and labor laws Congress has passed during the last 20 years. If you're planning to take legal action, find out more about:

   - The Equal Pay Act of 1963.
   - The Civil Rights Act of 1964.
   - The Age Discrimination in Employment Act of 1967.
   - The Occupational Safety and Health Act of 1970.

- The Federal Privacy Act of 1974.
- The Americans with Disabilities Act of 1990.
- The Family and Medical Leave Act of 1993.

Hopefully, this book has provided many ideas, methods and alternatives to help you manage your boss and turn bad-boss situations into positive ones before they reach the stage where legal action is called for.

Conclusion

A Final Word

If there's one motto you should keep in mind for the '90s, it's *change before you must!*

We're in the middle of a decade in which change is rampant. All of us are being asked to make fundamental changes in the way we think, plan and act.

In response, employers are placing a premium on the ability to learn and grow. Today's managers—in fact, *all* of today's staff people—are expected to be self-teachers and lifelong learners who learn what they must in order to sharpen and improve their performance.

Of course, "change before you must" doesn't mean "change the first thing that comes to mind." Effective change comes when you have thought long and hard about what needs to be changed, what benefits the change will bring, and how the process of change should be managed.

In what areas do you need to learn and grow? What skills do you need to acquire to prosper in the future? How can you acquire them? How will those new skills affect you?

How to Manage Your Boss

You may be asked to help your organization change the way it does business. Dreaming up new ways your company can realize its mission can be a profitable spare-time activity, especially if your company has a good record of rewarding employees for innovation. What can you do to help facilitate change in your organization? How can you help your organization add value to its services, and serve its customers better?

Your brain is your most powerful weapon in the process of change. Learn how to harness your brain power for your own and your organization's success. Improve your ability to solve puzzles and attack problems. Try to see old procedures in a new light.

If your brain is your most powerful weapon, your boss may be your most powerful ally. But your arsenal and your allies will only be useful if you manage them wisely. Change always comes more quickly than you think. Get ready for it now!

Index

How to Manage
Your Boss

Achievements, self-assessment, 28-29
Age Discrimination in Employment Act of 1967, The, 215
Americans with Disabilities Act of 1990, The, 216
Anger, 43-45
    bosses, 77-78
Anxiety, 53-54
Attitude, 76

Body language, 130-131
    negative, 130-131
    positive, 130
Bosses,
    angry, 77-78, 180-183
    charismatic, 183-185
    competitive, 185-187
    delegating, 187-189
    dependent, 189-190
    disorganized, 190-191
    effect of stress on, 64-65
    effective, 80-81
    emotions, 76-80
    fearful, 78-80
    getting to know, 69-84
    goals, 70-72
    incompetent, 193-195
    indifferent, 195-197
    intimidating, 197-198
    lifestyle, 83-84
    management style, 82-83
    moody, 198-199
    motivating, 199-201
    needs, 97-103
    off-site, 203-204
    parental, 204-206
    personal power, 16, 74

219

personal style, 81
power of position, 15-16, 73
power, 15-17, 72-74
rating, 85-95
"savior," 201-203
sexual harassment, 208-209
strengths and weaknesses, 74-76
substance abuse, 191-193
team-building, 210-211
time management styles, 59-61
tough, 180-183
warning signs of failure, 173-174

Caesar, 13
Chain of command, 14
Change, managing, 154-155
Charismatic bosses, 183-185
Civil Rights Act of 1964, The, 215
Communication, 155
   problems, 136-140
   with boss, 123-141
Competitive bosses, 185-187
Competitive Edge Profile, 146-152
Conflicts,
   with boss, 110
   work style, 120-122
Corporate structure, military, 13

Decision-making, rating your boss, 94
Delegating bosses, 187-189
Dependability, bosses' needs, 97-98
Dependent bosses, 189-190

Depression, 46-47
Disorganized bosses, 190-191
Duties and knowledge, rating your boss, 92
Duties, self-management, 34

Emotions, anger and depression, 43-47
Emotions,
   boss, 76-80
   boss's needs, 118-120
   managing, 41-55
   self-assessment, 41-42
   power, 17-19
   proactive, 11
Empowerment, 15
Equal Pay Act of 1963, The, 215
Essential, making yourself, 113-114

Family and Medical Leave Act of 1993, The, 216
Fear, 50-53
Fear, bosses, 78-80
Federal Privacy Act of 1974, The, 216
Flexibility, 37
Friendship, with boss, 156-157

Goals,
   boss's, 70-72
   long-term, 29, 31
   prioritizing, 30
   self-assessment, 29-32
   short-term, 29, 31
Grievances,
   filing, 213-214
   going public, 214-215

Incompetent bosses, 193-195
Indifferent bosses, 195-197
Information, 99
    rating your boss, 88
Intimidating bosses, 197-198

Joy, emotions, 47-48

Leadership, rating your boss, 93
Leaving your job, 174-176
Legal action, against bosses, 215
Lifestyle, bosses, 83-84
Listening, to boss, 124-127
Long-term goals, 29, 31
Loyalty, bosses' needs, 97-98

Management style,
    bosses, 82-83
    rating your boss, 86
Managing boss, benefits of, 10
Meetings,
    concluding, 132-133
    conducting, 130
    following up, 133
    performance review, 164-165
    preparing for, 129
    setting up, 128-128
    when not productive, 127-128
    with boss, 125ff
Memos,
    how to write, 135-136
    when not to send, 134
Military structure, business, 13
Moody bosses, 198-199
Motivating bosses, 199-201

Napoleon, 13
National Sleep Alert, 47
Need,
    of bosses, 97-103
    boss's emotional, 118-120
    boss's unreasonable, 120

Objectives,
    defining, 34-35
    self-management, 34
Occupational Safety and Health
    Act of 1970, The, 215
Off-site bosses, 203-204
Office politics, 25

Parental bosses, 204-206
Partnership, with boss, 108
Performance, 98-99
    evaluating, 156
    measuring, 34-35
Performance reviews, 159-170
    determining your worth, 163
    feedback, 162
    materials for, 162
    meeting, 164-165
    preparing for, 162-165
    top-down, 160
Personal Performance Contract,
    166ff, 168-169
Personal power, 16, 18-19
    boss, 74
Personal style, bosses, 82
Planning ability, rating your
    boss, 87
Power,
    employees, 17-19
    how to use, 19
Power of position, 15-16
    boss, 73
    employees, 18
Power pyramid, 13-14, 72
Proactive employees, 11

Rank, 14
Rating your boss, 85-95
 decision-making, 94
 delegation, 90
 duties and knowledge, 92
 information/communication, 88
 leadership, 93
 management style, 86
 planning ability, 87
 time management, 89
Respect, for boss, 101
Responsibilities, prioritizing, 35
Risks, 153-154

"Savior," bosses, 201-203
Self-assessment, 22-32
 achievements, 28-29
 goals, 29-32
 strengths and weaknesses, 25-26
 work habits, 23-25
Self-management, 33-39
 flexibility, 37
Self-trust, 49-50
Sexual harassment, 208-209
Shared authority, 14
Short-term goals, 29, 31
Sleep Disorders: America's Hidden Nightmare, 47
Solutions, 111
Strengths and weaknesses,

boss, 74-76
 performance reviews, 161
 self-assessment, 25-26
Stress, 41
 boss's, 100-101
 controlling, 63
 effect on bosses, 64-65
 good, 65
 time management, 62-65
Substance abuse, bosses, 191-193
Success,
 creating, 107-111
 ensuring boss's, 107
 strategies for, 113-122

Team-building, 38
 bosses, 210-211
Teaming, 15
Time management, 57-68
 boss's, 100
 rating your boss, 89
 self-assessment, 57-58
 stress, 62-65
Tough bosses, 180-183
Trust, 49-50

Whistle-blowing, grievances, 215
Work habits, self-assessment, 23-25
Work style, conflicts, 120-122